ACKNOWLEDGEMENTS

The Office of the United States Trade Representative (USTR) is responsible for the preparation of this report. U.S. Trade Representative Michael Froman gratefully acknowledges contributions of all USTR staff who contributed to the drafting and review of this report. Thanks are extended to partner Executive Branch agencies, including the U.S. Departments of Agriculture, Commerce, Labor, Justice, State, Transportation and Treasury, the U.S. Environmental Protection Agency, the U.S. Food and Drug Administration, the U.S. Consumer Product Safety Commission, and the Office of Management and Budget, as well as to the U.S. International Trade Commission.

In preparing the report, substantial information was solicited from U.S. embassies and from interested stakeholders.

April 2014

Table of Contents

I. FOREWORD

This year the USTR publishes its fifth annual *Report on Technical Barriers to Trade (TBT Report)*. This report was created to respond to the concerns of U.S. companies, farmers, ranchers, and manufacturers, which increasingly encounter nontariff trade barriers in the form of product standards, testing requirements, and other technical requirements as they seek to sell products and services around the world. As tariff barriers to industrial and agricultural trade have fallen, some standards-related measures have emerged as a key concern.

Governments, market participants, and other entities can use standards-related measures as an effective and efficient means of achieving legitimate commercial and policy objectives, such as protection of the environment, human health and safety. But when standards-related measures are outdated, overly burdensome, discriminatory, or otherwise inappropriate, these measures can reduce competition, stifle innovation, and create unnecessary technical barriers to trade. These kinds of measures can pose a particular problem for small and medium sized enterprises (SMEs), which often do not have the resources to address these problems on their own. USTR is committed to identifying and combating unwarranted technical barriers to U.S. exports, many of which are detailed in this report.

Since the last *TBT Report* was released, the United States has significantly advanced its efforts to resolve concerns with standards-related measures that act as unjustifiable barriers to trade and to prevent their emergence. USTR will continue its work to resolve and prevent standards-related trade concerns through new and existing cooperative initiatives in the World Trade Organization (WTO), Asia Pacific Economic Cooperation Forum (APEC), U.S. free trade agreements (FTAs), and other fora. In addition USTR will continue working to conclude on the negotiation of a modernized Technical Barriers to Trade (TBT) chapter in the Trans-Pacific Partnership (TPP) that builds on and strengthens TBT disciplines contained in the WTO Agreement on Technical Barriers to Trade (TBT Agreement). In addition, in June 2013, President Obama and European Union (EU) leaders launched negotiations on a comprehensive trade and investment agreement, the Transatlantic Trade and Investment Partnership (T-TIP). As conveyed in the February 2013 *United States-European Union High Level Working Group on Jobs and Growth (HLWG) Final Report*, the United States and the EU are committed to working together to open markets in goods, services and investment, reduce nontariff barriers, and address global trade issues of common concern. Both parties seek to build on the horizontal disciplines of the WTO TBT Agreement, establish ongoing mechanisms for improved dialogue and cooperation for addressing bilateral technical barriers to trade (TBT) issues, and pursue opportunities for greater regulatory compatibility with the objective of reducing unnecessary costs stemming from regulatory differences in specific sectors.

Again in 2014, USTR will engage vigorously with other agencies of the U.S. Government, as well as interested stakeholders, to press for tangible progress by U.S. trading partners in removing unwarranted or overly burdensome technical barriers. We will fully utilize our toolkit of bilateral, regional and multilateral agreements and mechanisms in order to dismantle unjustifiable barriers to safe, high quality U.S. industrial, consumer, and agricultural exports and strengthen the rules-based trading system. Recognizing that U.S. economic and employment recovery and growth continue to rely importantly on the strength of U.S. exports of goods, services, and agricultural products; we will be redoubling our efforts to ensure that the technical barriers that inhibit those exports are steadily diminished.

Ambassador Michael Froman
U.S. Trade Representative
April 2014

II. EXECUTIVE SUMMARY

The *2014 TBT Report* is a specialized report focused on significant foreign trade barriers in the form of product standards, technical regulations and testing, certification, and other procedures involved in determining whether products conform to standards and technical regulations and actions the United States is taking to address these barriers. These standards-related trade measures, which in World Trade Organization (WTO) terminology are known as "technical barriers to trade" (TBT), play a critical role in shaping the flow of global trade.

Standards-related measures serve an important function in facilitating international trade, including by enabling small and medium sized enterprises (SMEs) to obtain greater access to foreign markets. Standards-related measures also enable governments to pursue legitimate objectives such as protecting human health and the environment and preventing deceptive practices. But standards-related measures that are nontransparent, discriminatory, or otherwise unwarranted can act as significant barriers to U.S. trade. Such measures can pose a particular problem for SMEs, which often do not have the resources to address these problems on their own.

This report describes and advances U.S. efforts to identify and eliminate standards-related measures that act as significant barrier to U.S. trade. The report consists of the following key components:

•   An introduction to standards-related measures, including the genesis of this report and the growing importance of standards-related measures in international trade (*Section III*);[1]

•   An overview of standards-related trade obligations, in particular rules governing standards-related measures under the WTO Agreement on Technical Barriers to Trade (TBT Agreement) and U.S. free trade agreements (*Section IV*);

•   A description of the U.S. legal framework for implementing its standards-related trade obligations (*Section V*);

•   A discussion of standards, including the role of international standards in facilitating trade and fulfilling legitimate public policy objectives and Federal agencies' participation in standards development (*Section VI*);

•   An elaboration on conformity assessment procedures, including Federal agencies' use

---

[1] For readers seeking a deeper understanding of the specific topics covered in this report, references and hyperlinks to additional information are provided throughout the report. To access official documents of the WTO (such as those identified by the document symbol "G/TBT/…") go to https://docs.wto.org/dol2fe/Pages/FE_Search/FE_S_S005.aspx and click on "search" and enter the document symbol.

of conformity assessment and the possibility for international systems of conformity assessment to facilitate trade (*Section VII*);

- A description of how the U.S. Government identifies technical barriers to trade and the process of interagency and stakeholder consultation it employs to determine how to address them (*Section VIII*);

- An explanation of how the United States engages with its trading partners to address standards-related measures that act as barriers and prevent creation of new barriers through multilateral, regional, and bilateral channels, including the WTO's Committee on Technical Barriers to Trade (WTO TBT Committee) and cooperative activities under the Asia Pacific Economic Cooperation Forum (APEC) Subcommittee on Standards and Conformance, among others (*Section IX*);

- An identification and description of significant standards-related trade barriers currently facing U.S. exporters, along with U.S. Government initiatives to eliminate or reduce the impact of these barriers (Section XI) in 16 countries – Argentina, Brazil, China, Chile, Colombia, Ecuador, India, Indonesia, Korea, Malaysia, Mexico, Peru, Russia, Saudi Arabia, Taiwan, and Turkey – as well as the European Union (EU).

III. INTRODUCTION

Genesis of this Report

Shortly after taking office in 2009, President Obama reaffirmed America's commitment to ensuring the effective implementation and enforcement of the WTO's system of multilateral trade rules. The President vowed to pursue an aggressive and transparent program of defending U.S. rights and benefits under the rules-based trading system as a key element in his vision to restore trade's role in leading economic growth and promoting higher living standards. The President has also recognized that nontariff barriers have grown in significance for U.S. exporters seeking access to foreign markets. Two kinds of nontariff measures pose a particular challenge to U.S. exports: sanitary and phytosanitary (SPS) measures and standards-related measures.

Accordingly, in 2009 USTR created a new *SPS Report* and a *TBT Report*. These reports are intended to promote understanding of the process of identifying nontariff measures in the form of SPS and standards-related measures that act as significant barriers to U.S. exports; to provide a central focus for engagement by U.S. agencies in resolving trade concerns related to these nontariff barriers; and to document the actions underway to give greater transparency and confidence to American workers, producers, businesses, and other stakeholders regarding the actions this Administration is taking on their behalf.

The *TBT Report* is a specialized report addressing significant foreign barriers in the form of product standards, technical regulations, and conformity assessment procedures (standards- related measures). Prior to 2010, the *National Trade Estimate Report on Foreign Trade Barriers (NTE Report)* addressed standards-related measures.[2] By addressing significant foreign trade barriers in the form of standards-related measures, the *TBT Report* meets the requirements under Section 181 of the Trade Act of 1974, as amended, to report on significant foreign trade barriers with respect to standards-related measures. A separate report addressing significant foreign trade barriers in the form of SPS measures (*2014 Report on Sanitary and Phytosanitary Measures*) is being released in parallel to this report.

The *TBT Report* includes country reports that identify specific standards-related trade barriers

---

[2] In accordance with section 181 of the Trade Act of 1974 (the 1974 Trade Act) (codified at 19 U.S.C. § 2241), as amended by section 303 of the Trade and Tariff Act of 1984 (the 1984 Trade Act), section 1304 of the Omnibus Trade and Competitiveness Act of 1988 (the 1988 Trade Act), section 311 of the Uruguay Round Trade Agreements Act (1994 Trade Act), and section 1202 of the Internet Tax Freedom Act, the Office of the U.S. Trade Representative is required to submit to the President, the Senate Finance Committee, and appropriate committees in the House of Representatives, an annual report on significant foreign trade barriers. The statute requires an inventory of the most important foreign barriers affecting U.S. exports of goods and services, foreign direct investment by U.S. persons, and protection of intellectual property rights.

imposed or under consideration by certain U.S. trading partners. The report also includes general information on standards-related measures, the processes and procedures the United States uses to implement these measures domestically, and the tools the United States uses to address standards-related measures when they act as unnecessary barriers to trade. This general information is provided to assist the reader in understanding the issues and trade concerns described in the last two sections of the report, as well as the channels for resolving them. These last section reviews identify and describe significant standards-related trade barriers currently facing U.S. producers and businesses, along with U.S. Government initiatives to eliminate or reduce these barriers.

Like the *NTE Report*, the source of the information for the *TBT Report* includes stakeholder comments that USTR solicited through a notice published in the *Federal Register*, reports from U.S. embassies abroad and from other Federal agencies, and USTR's ongoing consultations with domestic stakeholders and trading partners. An appendix to this report includes a list of commenters that submitted comments in response to the *Federal Register* notice.

Central Focus in 2013

During 2013, the United States succeeded in persuading its trading partners to reduce or eliminate a variety of unwarranted standards-related barriers to trade identified in last year's report. The United States also continued to intensify its efforts to help other governments to avoid imposing unwarranted standards-related barriers to trade, particularly with respect to innovative technologies and new areas of regulation, and to strengthen their capacity to regulate properly and to promote good regulatory practices. In 2013, to encourage governments to eliminate and prevent unwarranted standards-related barriers to trade, the United States proposed new initiatives in key trade and economic forums, including in the WTO and the Asia Pacific Economic Cooperation Forum (APEC); launched negotiations for the Transatlantic Trade and Investment Partnership (T-TIP); and sought to conclude a Trans-Pacific Partnership (TPP) agreement.

Overview of Standards-Related Measures

Today, standards-related measures (standards, technical regulations, and conformity assessment procedures) play a critical role in shaping the flow of international trade. While tariffs still constitute an important source of distortions and economic costs, the relative role of tariffs in shaping international trade has declined due in large part to successful rounds of multilateral tariff reductions in the WTO and its predecessor, the General Agreement on Tariffs and Trade (GATT 1947). With tariff reductions, the role of nontariff barriers in international trade has become more prominent.

Broadly speaking, standards-related measures are documents and procedures that set out specific technical or other requirements for products or processes as well as procedures to ensure that these requirements are met. Among other things standards-related measures help:

- ensure the connectivity and compatibility of inputs sourced in different markets;

9

- manage the flow of product-related information through complex and increasingly global supply chains;

- organize manufacturing or other production processes around replicable routines and procedures to yield greater product quality assurance;

- achieve important regulatory and societal objectives, such as ensuring product safety, preventing deceptive practices, and protecting the environment; and

- promote more environmentally sound or socially conscious production methods.

Standards-related measures also play a vital role in enabling greater competition by conveying information to producers and consumers about the characteristics or performance of components and end products they purchase from a wide variety of suppliers. These measures also enable more widespread access to technical innovations. Standards-related measures can offer particularly pronounced benefits to SMEs from this perspective. Uniform standards and product testing procedures established under a common set of technical requirements that producers can rely on in manufacturing components and end products, can facilitate the diffusion of technology and innovation, contribute to increasing buyer-seller confidence, and assist SMEs to participate in global supply chains.

Conversely, outdated, overly burdensome, discriminatory, or otherwise inappropriate standards-related measures can reduce competition, stifle innovation, and create unnecessary obstacles to trade. Even when standards-related measures are used appropriately, firms – particularly SMEs – can face significant challenges in accessing information about, and complying with, diverse and evolving technical requirements in major export markets. This is particularly the case when technical requirements change rapidly or differ markedly across markets.

Thus, while standards-related measures can be an effective and efficient means of achieving legitimate commercial and policy objectives, policy makers, industry officials, and other stakeholders must also confront an important question: how to ensure that standards-related measures facilitate innovation, competition, consumer and environmental protection, and other public policy objectives, without creating unnecessary obstacles to trade? As supply chains grow increasingly complex, governments and other stakeholders must also address the question of how to better align standards and technical requirements across jurisdictions and markets as a means to facilitate the flow of goods across borders, reduce costs associated with complying with different standards and technical regulations across jurisdictions and markets, and enhance governments' ability to achieve important public policy objectives.

The rules, procedures, and opportunities for engagement that international, regional, and bilateral trade agreements establish serve as an important foundation for addressing many of these questions. The TBT Agreement is the principal agreement establishing multilateral rules governing standards-related measures. (Box 1 lays out definitions provided under the TBT Agreement for standards-related measures.) U.S. FTAs establish additional rules with respect to these measures with specific trading partners. The TBT Agreement's rules are vital in setting the terms on which the United States engages with its trading partners on standards-related measures, and U.S. FTAs build on these rules in important ways. *(These agreements are described in more detail in Section IV below.)*

A broad and active agenda of U.S. engagement on many fronts is needed to ensure that foreign standards-related measures do not impose unwarranted barriers to trade. USTR leads Federal Government policy deliberations on these measures through the interagency Trade Policy Staff Committee (TPSC).[3] U.S. activities in the WTO are at the forefront of USTR's efforts to prevent and resolve trade concerns arising from standards-related measures. Coordinating with relevant agencies through the TPSC, USTR engages with other governments in many fora, including those established by U.S. FTAs and through regional and multilateral organizations, such as the WTO, APEC and the Organization for Economic Cooperation and Development (OECD). USTR also raises standards-related issues in bilateral dialogues with U.S. trading partners. These efforts are designed to ensure that U.S. trading partners adhere to internationally agreed rules governing these measures and to reduce or eliminate unnecessary measures of this kind that can create barriers for U.S. producers and businesses.

Box 1. Key Definitions in the WTO Agreement on Technical Barriers to Trade

Technical regulation

Document which lays down product characteristics or their related processes and production methods, including the applicable administrative provisions, with which compliance is mandatory. It may also include or deal exclusively with terminology, symbols, packaging, marking, or labeling requirements as they apply to a product, process, or production method.

Standard

Document approved by a recognized body, that provides, for common and repeated use, rules, guidelines, or characteristics for products or related processes and production methods, with which compliance is not mandatory. It may also include or deal exclusively with terminology, symbols, packaging, marking, or labeling requirements as they apply to a product, process, or production method.

Conformity assessment procedures

Any procedure used, directly or indirectly, to determine that relevant requirements in technical regulations or standards are fulfilled.

Explanatory note: Conformity assessment procedures include, *inter alia*, procedures for sampling, testing and inspection; evaluation, verification and assurance of conformity; registration, accreditation, and approval as well as their combinations.

Source: Annex 1 of the TBT Agreement

Note: These definitions apply only with respect to products and related processes and production methods, not to services

---

[3] http://www.ustr.gov/about-us/executive-branch-agencies-trade-policy-staff-committee-and-trade-policy-review-group

IV. OVERVIEW OF TRADE OBLIGATIONS ON STANDARDS-RELATED MEASURES

WTO Agreement on Technical Barriers to Trade

The *WTO Agreement on Technical Barriers to Trade (TBT Agreement)* contains rules that help ensure that standards-related measures serve legitimate objectives, are transparent, and do not create unnecessary obstacles to trade.[4] The *TBT Agreement* establishes rules on developing, adopting, and applying voluntary product standards and mandatory technical regulations as well as conformity assessment procedures (such as testing or certification) used to determine whether a particular product meets such standards or regulations. These rules help distinguish legitimate standards-related measures from protectionist measures, and ensure that testing and other conformity assessment procedures are fair and reasonable.

The *TBT Agreement* recognizes that WTO Members have the right to prepare, adopt, and apply standards-related measures necessary to protect human health, safety and the environment at the levels they consider appropriate and to achieve other legitimate objectives. At the same time, the *TBT Agreement* imposes obligations regarding the development and application of those measures. For example, the *TBT Agreement* requires governments to develop standards-related measures through transparent processes, and to base these measures on relevant international standards (where effective and appropriate). The *TBT Agreement* also prohibits measures that discriminate against imported products or create unnecessary obstacles to trade. The *TBT Agreement* contains a *Code of Good Practice for the Preparation, Adoption, and Application of Standards (Code).* The Code applies to the preparation, adoption, and application of voluntary standards and is open to acceptance by any standardizing body located in the territory of any WTO Member, including government and non-governmental bodies. *(Box 2 outlines the key disciplines of the TBT Agreement.)*

Box 2. Key principles and provisions of the *TBT Agreement*

Non-discrimination: The *TBT Agreement* states that "in respect of their technical regulations, products imported from the territory of any Member [shall] be accorded treatment no less favorable than that accorded to like products of national origin and to like products originating in any other country." (Art. 2.1) The Agreement requires Members to ensure that "conformity assessment procedures are prepared, adopted and applied so as to grant access for suppliers of like products originating in the territories of other Members under conditions no less favorable than those accorded to suppliers of like products of national origin or originating in any other country, in a comparable situation." (Art. 5.1.1) The Agreement also requires that Members ensure that related fees are equitable (Art. 5.2.5) and that they respect the confidentiality of information about the results of conformity assessment procedures for imported products in the same way they do for domestic products. (Art. 5.2.4)

Avoidance of unnecessary obstacles to trade: When preparing or applying a technical regulation, a Member must ensure that the regulation is not more trade restrictive than necessary to fulfill the Member's legitimate objective.

---

[4] http://www.wto.org/english/docs_e/legal_e/17-tbt_e.htm

12

(Art. 2.2) The obligation to avoid unnecessary obstacles to trade applies also to conformity assessment procedures. They must not be stricter than necessary to provide adequate confidence that products conform to the applicable requirements. (Art. 5.1.2)

Better alignment of technical regulations, standards, and conformity assessment procedures: The Agreement calls on Members to use relevant international standards, or the relevant parts of them, as a basis for their technical regulations, and to use relevant international recommendations and guides, or relevant portions of them, as the basis for their conformity assessment procedures. The Agreement, however, does not require the use of relevant international standards, guides, and recommendations if they would be ineffective or inappropriate to fulfill the Member's "legitimate objectives." (Arts. 2.4 and 5.4) In addition, Members should participate "within the limits of their resources" in the preparation by international standardization bodies, of international standards for products for which they either have adopted, or expect to adopt, technical regulation, and in the elaboration of international guides and recommendations for conformity assessment procedures. (Art.2.6 and 5.5)

Use of performance-based requirements: Whenever appropriate, product requirements should be set in terms of performance rather than design or descriptive characteristics. (Art. 2.8)

International systems of conformity assessment: Members shall, whenever practicable, formulate and adopt international systems for conformity assessment and become Members thereof or participate therein. (Art. 9.1)

Acceptance of technical regulations as equivalent: Alongside promoting better alignment of technical regulations, the Agreement encourages Members to accept technical regulations that other Members adopt as "equivalent" to their own if these regulations adequately fulfill the objectives of their own regulations. (Art. 2.7)

Mutual recognition of conformity assessment: The Agreement requires each Member to recognize "whenever possible" the results of conformity assessment procedures (*e.g,* test results or certifications), provided the Member is satisfied that those procedures offer an assurance of conformity that is equivalent as its own. (Art. 6.1) (Without such recognition, products might have to be tested twice, first by the exporting country and then by the importing country.) The Agreement recognizes that Members may need to consult in advance to arrive at a "mutually satisfactory understanding" regarding the competences of their respective conformity assessment bodies. (Art. 6.1) The Agreement also encourages Members to enter into negotiations to conclude agreements providing for the mutual recognition of each other's conformity assessment results (*i.e.,* mutual recognition agreements (MRAs)). (Art. 6.3)

Transparency: To help ensure transparency, the Agreement requires Members to publish a notice at an early stage and notify other Members through the WTO Secretariat when it proposes to adopt a technical regulation or conformity assessment procedure and to include in the notification a brief indication of the purpose of the proposed measure. These obligations apply whenever a relevant international standard, guide, or recommendation does not exist or the technical content of a proposed technical regulation or conformity assessment procedure is not in accordance with the technical content of relevant international standards, guides, or recommendations. In such circumstances, Members must allow "reasonable time" for other Members to comment on proposed technical regulations and conformity assessment procedures, which the WTO TBT Committee has recommended be "at least 60 days" (G/TBT/26), and take comments it receives from other Members into account. (Art. 2.9 and 5.6) The Agreement establishes a Code of Good Practice that is applicable to voluntary standards and directs Members and standardizing bodies that have accepted it to publish every six months a work program containing the standards it is currently preparing and give interested parties at least 60 days to comment on a draft standard; once the standard is adopted it must be promptly published. (Annex 3) The Agreement also requires that all final technical regulations and conformity assessment procedures be promptly published. (Art. 2.11 and 5.8) In addition, the Agreement requires each Member to establish an inquiry point to answer all reasonable questions from other Members and interested parties and to provide documents relating to technical regulations, standards, and conformity assessment procedures adopted or proposed within its territory. (Art. 10.1)

Technical assistance: The Agreement calls on Members to provide technical assistance to other Members. (Art. 11) Technical assistance can be provided to help developing country Members with respect to such matters as preparing technical regulations, establishing national standardizing bodies, participating in international standardization bodies, and establishing bodies to assess conformity with technical regulations.

Enforcement and dispute settlement: The Agreement establishes the TBT Committee as the major forum for WTO Members to consult on matters relating to the operation of the Agreement, including specific trade concerns about measures that Members have proposed or adopted. (Art. 13) The TBT Agreement provides for disputes under the Agreement to be resolved under the auspices of the WTO Dispute Settlement Body and in accordance with the terms of the WTO's Dispute Settlement Understanding. (Art. 14)

Other: As noted above, the Agreement sets out a Code for preparing, adopting, and applying voluntary standards. (Annex 3) Standardizing bodies that Members establish at the central level of government must comply with the Code, and Members must take reasonable measures to ensure that local government and private sector standardizing bodies within their territories also accept and comply with the Code. (Art. 4.1) The Code is open to acceptance by any standardizing body in the territory of a WTO Member, including private sector bodies as well as public sector bodies. The Code requires Members and other standardizing bodies that have accepted it to adhere to obligations similar to those for technical regulations, for example, to ensure that the standards they adopt do not create unnecessary obstacles to trade and are based on relevant international standards, except where ineffective or inappropriate.

Note: The OECD and WTO have also developed summaries of the *TBT Agreement*. See Trade Policy Working Paper No. 58, Do Bilateral and Regional Approaches for Reducing Technical Barriers to Trade Converge Towards The Multilateral Trading System? (OECD (TAD/TC/WP (2007)12/FINAL), WTO Trade Gateway, and TBT Committee reports and recommendations.

Access to information on product related technical requirements is critical for facilitating trade. Producers, growers, manufacturers, and other supply chain participants need to know the requirements with which their products must comply in order to sell them in prospective markets. The *TBT Agreement*, therefore, requires every WTO Member to establish a national inquiry point that is able to answer reasonable questions from other Members and interested parties concerning the Member's proposed or existing measures and provides relevant documents, as appropriate. It also requires each WTO Member to ensure that all standards- related measures that it adopts are promptly published or otherwise made publicly available.

The *TBT Agreement* requires each WTO Member to provide other Members the opportunity to participate in the development of mandatory standards-related measures, which helps to ensure that standards-related measures do not become unnecessary obstacles to trade.[5] In particular, the *TBT Agreement* requires each Member to publish a notice in advance that it proposes to adopt a technical regulation or conformity assessment procedure.[6] It also requires each WTO Member to notify proposed technical regulations and conformity assessment procedures to the WTO so that other WTO Members may comment on them in writing. WTO Members are required, without discrimination, to take into account these written comments, plus the results of any requested, discussions of those comments, when finalizing the measures.[7]

---

[5] Depending on the WTO Member's domestic processes, interested parties may participate directly in that Member's process for developing new standards-related measures, for example, by submitting written comments to the Member, or indirectly by working with their own governments to submit comments.

[6] WTO Members typically do this by publishing a notice in an official journal of national circulation or on a government website that they propose to adopt a technical regulation or conformity assessment procedure or by publishing the full text of the draft measure.

[7] The obligations described in this paragraph apply to measures that have a significant effect on trade and are not based on relevant international standards, guides, or recommendations or in circumstances where relevant international

In 2013 alone, WTO Members notified 1,626 new or revised technical regulations and conformity assessment procedures, as well as submitted 467 addenda and 42 corrigenda to previous notifications. Since entry into force of the *Marrakesh Agreement Establishing the World Trade Organization (WTO Agreement)*[8] on January 1, 1995, up to December 31, 2013, 17,418 notifications along with 3,150 addenda and 524 corrigenda to these notifications have been made by 121 Members. Box 3 shows the number of notifications yearly since 1995.[9]

Box 3. Number of TBT Notifications since 1995[10]

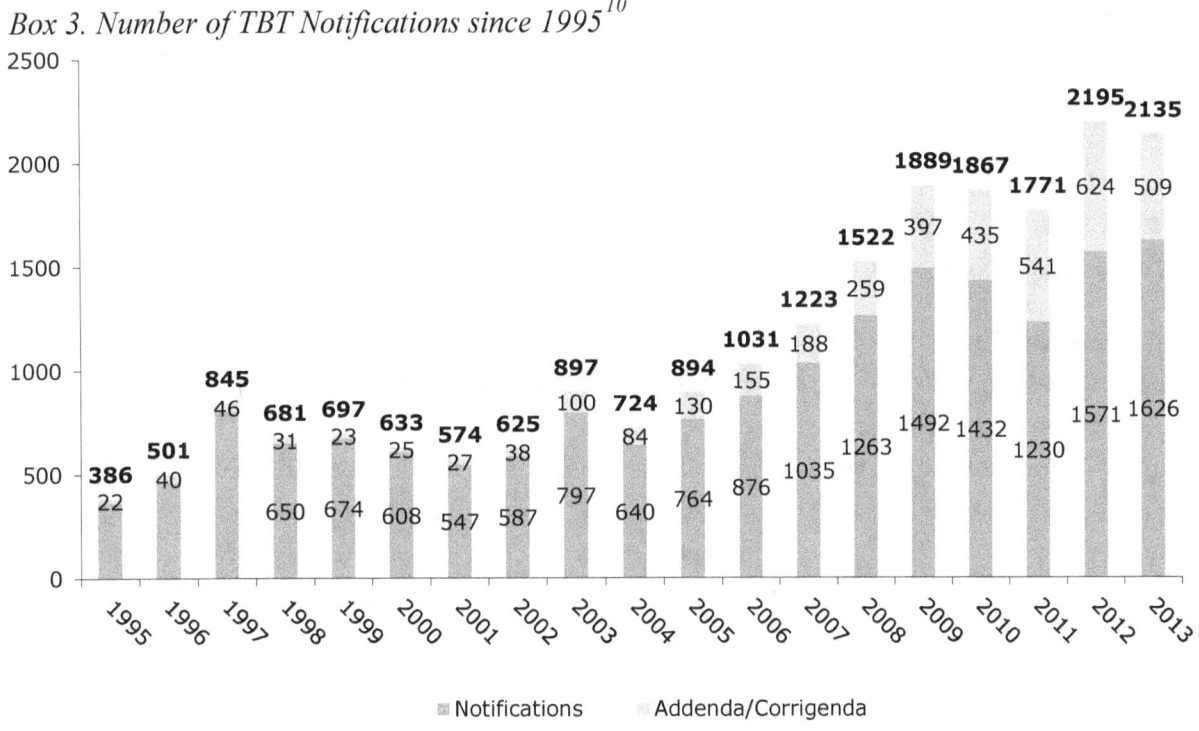

Article 13 of the *TBT Agreement* establishes a "Committee on Technical Barriers to Trade" to oversee the operation and implementation of the *TBT Agreement*. The WTO TBT Committee is open to participation by all 159 WTO Members. The WTO TBT Committee is one of over a dozen

---

standards, guides, or recommendations do not exist. In many instances, however, Members, including the United States, notify proposed technical regulations and conformity assessment procedures regardless of whether they are based on relevant international standards.

[8] The TBT Agreement is one of several agreements, understandings and decisions comprising the WTO Agreement.

[9] WTO Members notify new measures, as well as addenda and corrigenda to previously notified measures. An addendum alerts WTO Members that substantive or technical changes have been made to a measure that has been previously notified. A corrigendum conveys editorial or administrative corrections to a previous notification. Many Members also notify adopted technical regulations and conformity assessment procedures (regardless of whether or not they are based on relevant international standards).

[10] Number of TBT Notifications since 1995 found in "Nineteenth Annual Review of the Implementation and Operation of the TBT Agreement (G/TBT/33)."

standing bodies (others include the Committees on Import Licensing, Antidumping Practices, and Rules of Origin, for example) that report to the WTO Council for Trade in Goods. The activities of the WTO TBT Committee are described in detail below.

Operation of the TBT Agreement

The TBT Agreement sets out rules covering standards-related measures developed and implemented by disparate bodies (central and local governmental agencies; inter-governmental entities; and non-governmental, national, and international standardizing organizations). WTO Members' central government authorities have primary responsibility for ensuring compliance with the TBT Agreement, including by taking reasonable measures to ensure that local and non-governmental bodies, such as private sector standards developing organizations, comply with the relevant provisions. Further, each WTO Member must inform the WTO TBT Committee of the laws, policies, and procedures it has adopted to implement and administer the TBT Agreement.[11]

The quality and coherence of these laws, policies, and procedures – as well as how they are put into practice – influence the extent to which standards-related measures in any particular country are transparent, non-discriminatory, and avoid creating unnecessary obstacles to trade, as the TBT Agreement requires. Sound mechanisms for internal coordination among a WTO Member's trade, regulatory, and standards officials are critical to ensuring that the Member effectively implements the TBT Agreement. When interested agencies and officials coordinate their efforts in developing standards-related measures, it makes it more likely that the government will consider alternative technical specifications that may reduce any adverse effects on trade while still fulfilling the measure's objective.

Further, when governments take account of how the products they propose to regulate are traded in foreign markets, it can actually make the measures they adopt more effective in fulfilling their objectives. The effectiveness of a WTO Member's internal coordination also often determines the extent to which it is able to resolve specific trade concerns raised by other Members. Accordingly, in some developing countries, ineffective internal coordination and a lack of established procedures for developing standards-related measures are a key concern. For these countries, technical assistance or cooperative efforts to improve internal coordination can be vital in helping U.S. exporters sell into these markets.

The WTO TBT Committee conducts triennial reviews of systemic issues affecting WTO Members' policies and procedures for implementing specific obligations.[12] In the course of these reviews, Members adopt specific recommendations and decisions, and lay out a forward looking work program to strengthen the implementation and operation of the TBT Agreement. To advance their understanding of systemic issues, Members share experiences and participate in special events and

---

[11] See G/TBT/GEN/1/Rev.11 for a list of Members' submissions on the measures they have taken to implement and administer the TBT Agreement.

[12] The Committee's work on the outcome of the most recent triennial review is discussed in Section IX of this report.

regional workshops to explore topics in depth. In recent years, WTO TBT Committee events have covered good regulatory practice, conformity assessment, transparency, the role of international standards in development, and regulatory cooperation.

In addition to its triennial reviews and the related special events and workshops, the WTO TBT Committee also meets three times a year. At these meetings, Members may raise any specific trade concern regarding standards-related measures that other WTO Members have proposed or adopted. The Committee's discussion of these concerns can help to clarify the technical aspects of the measures concerned, promote greater understanding of how the measures might affect trade, and perhaps even help to resolve the concerns. In 2013, WTO Members raised over 73 specific trade concerns in the WTO TBT Committee, including, for example, concerns regarding measures relating to managing hazards arising from use of chemicals, labeling and other nonsafety requirements relating to food products, and duplicative or redundant testing requirements on a wide variety of goods such as toys and medical devices. WTO Members have underscored the importance of the WTO TBT Committee's regular discussions of specific trade concerns, and agreed that the WTO TBT Committee's work has helped to clarify and resolve trade issues between WTO Members.[13]

Box 4 shows the number of specific trade concerns WTO Members have raised in the WTO TBT Committee since 1995. The general increase in concerns raised over the past few years reflects several factors, including an increase in the number of proposed measures that WTO Members have notified to the WTO, a heightened focus on standards-related activities, increased concern that these measures may be used as a form of disguised protectionism, and an increasing perception that discussions in the WTO TBT Committee, as well as bilateral discussions on the margins of Committee meetings, can lead to results in addressing trade concerns. For a full accounting of the concerns raised in the Committee since 1995, see G/TBT/31.

---

[13] See the discussion of the Operation of the Committee in the *Fifth Triennial Review of the Operation and Implementation of the Agreement on Technical Barriers to Trade under Article 15.4*, G/TBT/26.

Box 4. Number of specific trade concerns[14]

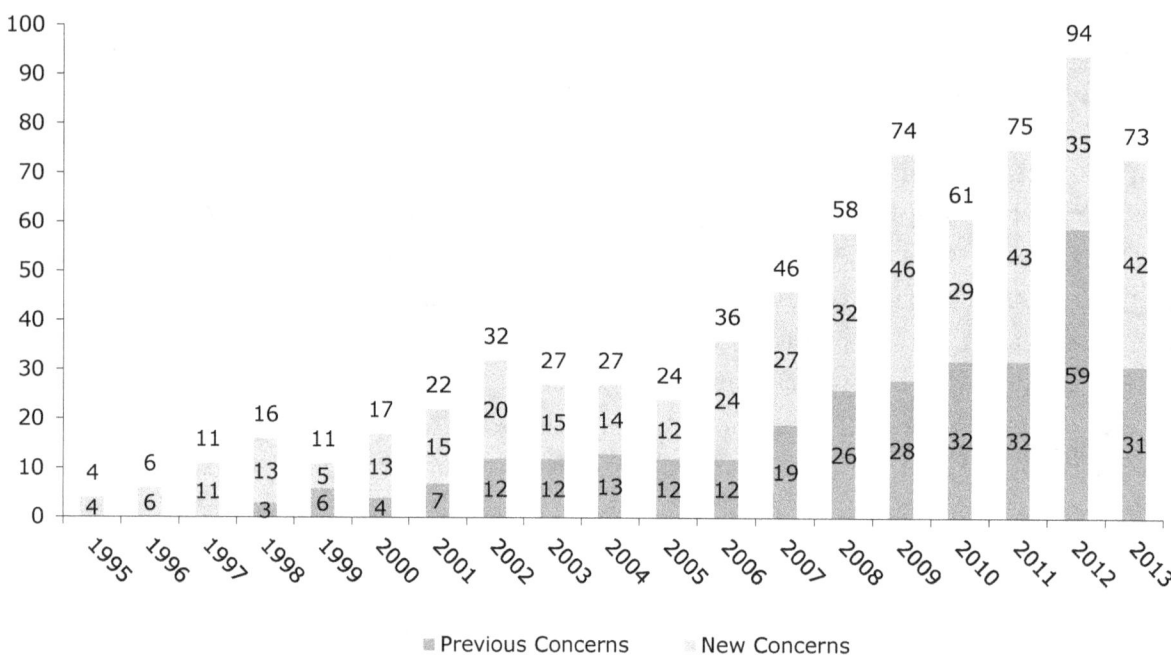

In recent years, the WTO TBT Committee has implemented procedures to streamline the discussion of specific trade concerns during its meetings and avoid unnecessary repetition. While addressing specific trade concerns is core to the WTO TBT Committee's responsibility in monitoring how well WTO Members are implementing the TBT Agreement, some exchanges on unresolved issues have become protracted, leaving less time for the WTO TBT Committee to address the cross-cutting or systemic issues needed to prevent and resolve trade issues. In 2012, the WTO TBT Committee agreed to use informal "thematic" discussions on the margins of its meetings in 2013, in order to sharpen focus and make progress on key systemic issues. In 2013, the WTO TBT Committee held thematic discussions on standards and good regulatory practices on March 5; on good regulatory practices and inquiry point operations on June 19; and on conformity assessment procedures, special and differential treatment, and technical assistance on October 29.

Standards-Related Provisions in U.S. Free Trade Agreements

In U.S. FTAs, the parties reaffirm their commitment to the TBT Agreement. U.S. FTAs build on the disciplines in the TBT Agreement in important ways, including by providing for greater transparency, establishing mechanisms for more in depth consultation on specific trade concerns,

---

[14] Number of specific trade concerns raised since 1995, found in "Nineteenth Annual Review of the Implementation and Operation of the TBT Agreement (G/TBT/33)."

and facilitating cooperation and coordination with FTA partners on systemic issues. As a result, the U.S. approach to standards-related measures in its FTAs is commonly referred to as "TBT plus."[15] For example, recent FTAs require each party to allow persons of the other party to participate in the development of standards, technical regulations and conformity assessment procedures. Moreover, each party is required to permit persons of the other party to participate in the development of these measures on terms no less favorable than it accords its own persons.

U.S. FTAs also contain a variety of other substantive obligations that go beyond those in the *TBT Agreement*. For example, U.S. FTAs require FTA partners to accredit or otherwise recognize U.S. testing and certification bodies under no less favorable terms than FTA partners accord their own testing and certification bodies. Recent U.S. FTAs, as well as the earlier *North American Free Trade Agreement (NAFTA)*, also build in mechanisms (such as special committees) for closer and more enduring engagement and cooperation on standards-related measures. These mechanisms can prevent specific trade concerns from arising and assist the FTA governments in resolving emerging problems.

By enhancing understanding of each party's respective rulemaking processes and standards and conformance processes, these consultative mechanisms can enable early identification of potential trade problems and provide opportunities for the FTA partners to discuss technical alternatives before a measure is finalized.[16] The provisions in U.S. FTAs that provide for more timely and robust consultations and participation, enhance the notifications process, and provide for direct bilateral engagement on notified measures are particularly important in this regard. These consultative mechanisms can provide a channel for peer to peer capacity building activities with FTA partners whose standards and conformance processes may be underdeveloped or otherwise in need of improvement.

At the same time, U.S. FTAs provide mechanisms through which FTA partners can reduce the negative effects on their bilateral trade stemming from unnecessary differences in their regulatory regimes. Several U.S. FTAs also contain provisions designed to encourage FTA partners to accept each other's regulations as equivalent to their own, where appropriate.

Lastly, recent U.S. FTAs provide strong support for the *U.S. Standards Strategy* – which establishes a framework for developing voluntary product standards – by formally recognizing the *WTO TBT Committee's 2000 Decision on Principles for the Development of International Standards*.[17] The

---

[15] For a discussion of agreements that promote divergence from multilateral approaches (or "TBT minus") see Trade Policy Working Paper No. 58, *Do Bilateral and Regional Approaches for Reducing Technical Barriers to Trade Converge towards the Multilateral Trading System?* (OECD (TAD/TC/WP (2007)12/FINAL).

[16] See, for example, G/TBT/W/317 for a discussion of the cooperative standards-related work on automobiles, chemicals, food, energy, and other issues under the NAFTA.

[17] Decision on Principles for the Development of International Standards, Guides and Recommendations with Relation to Articles 2, 5 and Annex 3 of the TBT Agreement, contained in document G/TBT/1/Rev.11.

U.S. experience with the 2000 Committee Decision is described at length in G/TBT/W/305. *(These issues are discussed in more detail in Section VI below.)*

Box 5. Key Standards-Related Provisions in U.S. Free Trade Agreements

The United States has concluded FTAs with a number of countries. While each agreement is unique, many of these FTAs share common provisions relating to standards-related measures. This box summarizes standards-related provisions common to U.S. FTAs with Australia, Bahrain, Central America and the Dominican Republic, Chile, Colombia, Korea, Morocco, Oman, Panama, and Peru.

Affirmation of the TBT Agreement: The FTAs reaffirm the parties' obligations under the TBT Agreement and use the TBT Agreement's definitions of key terms, such as technical regulation, standard, and conformity assessment procedures.

International standards: The FTAs require FTA partners to apply the principles of the 2000 Committee Decision in determining whether an international standard, guide, or recommendation exists.

Conformity assessment procedures: The FTAs recognize the variety of mechanisms that exist for facilitating acceptance of each other's conformity assessment procedures, and they list specific examples of those mechanisms. The agreements also call for FTA partners to intensify their exchange of information regarding these mechanisms; require an FTA partner to explain when it will not accept, or negotiate agreements to accept, another partner's conformity assessment results; call for FTA partners to recognize conformity assessment bodies in another partner's territory on a national treatment basis; and require FTA partners to explain any refusal to recognize another party's conformity assessment body.

Transparency: The FTAs expand upon transparency obligations provided for in the TBT Agreement. For example, US FTAs with Colombia, Peru and Korea provide that each party shall permit persons from the other party to participate in the development of standards-related measures on terms no less favorable than those it accords to its own persons and require parties (1) to notify proposed technical regulations even where those regulations are based on relevant international standards; (2) to notify proposals for technical regulations or conformity assessment procedures directly to the other party; (3) to include in notifications of proposed technical regulations and conformity assessment procedures the objectives of the proposed measure and the proposed measure's rationale or how the measure meets those objectives; (4) to provide interested parties as well as the FTA partner a meaningful opportunity to comment on the proposed measure; (5) to allow at least 60 days for comment; (6) to provide responses to significant comments received no later than the time a final measure is published; and (7) to provide additional information about the objectives when requested.

Cooperation: The FTAs provide for FTA partners to intensify their joint work on technical regulations, standards, and conformity assessment procedures. They also urge parties to identify bilateral initiatives for specific issues or sectors.

Information Exchange: The FTAs call on each FTA partner to provide information or explanations regarding proposed measures within a reasonable period following a request from another FTA partner.

Administration: Each FTA creates its own committee or subcommittee to monitor application of the agreement's provisions, address specific issues that arise under the agreement, enhance cooperation, and exchange information on pertinent developments.

Note: For more information, see http://www.ustr.gov/trade-agreements/free-trade-agreements.

V. U.S. STATUTORY AND ADMINISTRATIVE FRAMEWORK FOR IMPLEMENTING STANDARDS-RELATED TRADE OBLIGATIONS

The United States maintains a robust system to support implementation of its trade obligations on standards-related measures through strong central management of its regulatory regime, an effective interagency trade policy mechanism, and public consultation. The legal framework for implementing U.S. obligations under the *TBT Agreement* and standards-related provisions in U.S. FTAs includes the *Administrative Procedure Act of 1946* (APA) and the *Trade Agreements Act of 1979* (TAA).[18] The APA establishes a process of public participation in rulemakings by U.S. agencies through a system of notice and comment. The TAA prohibits Federal agencies from engaging in any standards-related activity that creates unnecessary obstacles to trade and directs them to consider the use of international standards in rulemaking.

The TAA establishes USTR as the lead agency within the Federal Government for coordinating and developing international trade policy regarding standards-related activities, as well as in discussions and negotiations with foreign governments on standards-related matters. In carrying out this responsibility, USTR is required to inform and consult with Federal agencies having expertise in the matters under discussion and negotiation. The TAA also directs the U.S. Secretaries of Commerce and Agriculture to keep abreast of international standards activities, to identify those activities that may substantially affect U.S. commerce, and to inform, consult, and coordinate with USTR with respect to international standards-related activities.

The APA provides the foundation for transparency and accountability in developing Federal regulations. The APA requires agencies to undertake a notice and comment process open to all members of the public, both foreign and domestic, for rulemakings, and to take these comments into account in the final rule.[19] In accordance with the APA, agencies publish proposed technical regulations and conformity assessment procedures in the *Federal Register* and solicit comments

---

[18] The standards-related provisions of the TAA are codified at United States Code, Title 19, Chapter 13, Subchapter II, Technical Barriers to Trade (Standards).

[19] The term "rule" refers to "an agency statement of general or particular applicability and future effect designed to implement, interpret, or prescribe law or policy...." 5 U.S.C. § 551(4). "Rule making" means the "agency process for formulating, amending, or repealing a rule...." 5 U.S.C. § 551(5). These definitions include rules or rulemakings regarding technical regulations and conformity assessment procedures. The APA makes exceptions for urgent matters, allowing Federal agencies to omit notice and comment, for example, where they find that notice and public procedures are impracticable or contrary to the public interest. 5 U.S.C. § 553(b)(3).

from the public through notices published in the *Federal Register*. To fulfill WTO obligations to notify proposed technical regulations and conformity assessment procedures, the National Institute of Standards and Technology (NIST) in the U.S. Department of Commerce serves as the U.S. notification authority and inquiry point for purposes of the TBT Agreement. The U.S. inquiry point reviews the *Federal Register* and other materials on a daily basis and notifies the WTO of technical regulations and conformity assessment procedures that agencies propose to adopt.

The foundation for central regulatory review is *Executive Order 12866 Regulatory Planning and Review* (E.O. 12866) and the implementing guidance of the Office and Management and Budget (OMB) *Circular A-4*. E.O. 12866 lays out the regulatory philosophy, principles, and actions that guide Federal agencies in planning, developing, and reviewing Federal regulations. E.O. 12866 and Circular A-4 are the primary basis on which good regulatory practice (GRP) has been integrated into the Federal regulatory structure. These practices ensure openness, transparency, and accountability in the regulatory process, and, as a result, help ensure that the United States fulfills key *TBT Agreement* and U.S. FTA obligations. GRP,[20] such as that embodied in E.O. 12866 and Circular A-4, enables government agencies to achieve their public policy objectives efficiently and effectively. GRP is also critical in reducing the possibility that governments will adopt standards-related measures that create unnecessary obstacles to trade.

Under the procedures set out in E.O. 12866, prior to adopting any significant regulatory action (*e.g.,* a proposed technical regulation), Federal agencies must submit it for review to OMB. Significant regulatory actions are defined to include any regulatory action that is likely to result in a rule that may:

1. have an annual impact on the U.S. economy of $100 million or more or adversely affect in a material way the economy, a sector of the economy, productivity, competition, jobs, the environment, public health or safety, or sub-federal governments;

2. create a serious inconsistency or otherwise interfere with an action taken or planned by another agency;

3. materially alter the budget impact of entitlements, grants, user fees or loan programs or the rights and obligations of their recipients; or

---

[20] For a discussion of good regulatory practices from the perspective of APEC and the OECD, see:

APEC, "*Information Notes on Good Practice for Technical Regulation,*" September 2000.

OECD, *Cutting Red Tape: National Strategies for Administrative Simplification.* Paris, 2006.

OECD, *Background Document on Oversight Bodies for Regulatory Reform*. Paris: OECD, 2007.

OECD, *Regulatory Impact Analyses: Best Practices in OECD Countries.* Paris: OECD, 1997.

OECD, *Regulatory Performance: Ex post Evaluation of Regulatory Policies*. Paris: OECD, 2003.

OECD and APEC, *APEC-OECD Integrated Checklist on Regulatory Reform.* Mexico City, 2005.

4. raise novel legal or policy issues.

For those significant rules that are determined by OMB to fall within the first category, OMB requires the agency to also provide an assessment of the benefits and costs of the regulation, including with respect to the efficient function of the economy and private markets, health and safety, the environment, and other alternatives that are potentially effective and reasonably feasible. OMB also reviews Federal agencies' proposed regulatory actions and consults with USTR and other agencies as needed. This review is designed to ensure, inter alia, that proposed regulatory actions are not duplicative or inconsistent with other planned or existing Federal regulatory actions, are consistent with U.S. international trade obligations, and take into account the trade impact of proposed regulatory actions. At the conclusion of this process, OMB provides guidance to the pertinent agency to ensure that its regulatory actions are consistent with applicable law, Presidential priorities, and E.O. 12866's regulatory principles.

On January 18, 2011, President Obama issued *Executive Order 13563 – Improving Regulation and Regulatory Review* (E.O. 13563), which reaffirms and supplements E.O. 12866. E.O. 13563 states that "[the U.S.] regulatory system must protect public health, welfare, safety, and our environment while promoting economic growth, innovation, competitiveness, and job creation. It must allow for public participation and an open exchange of ideas. It must promote predictability and reduce uncertainty. It must identify and use the best, most innovative and least burdensome tools for achieving regulatory ends. It must take into account benefits and costs, both quantitative and qualitative." E.O. 13563 sets out certain regulatory principles, as well as new requirements designed to promote public participation, improve regulatory integration and innovation, increase flexibility, ensure scientific integrity, and increase retrospective analysis of existing rules.

On May 12, 2012, President Obama issued *Executive Order 13610 Identifying and Reducing Regulatory Burdens* (E.O. 13610), which requires agencies to conduct retrospective analyses of existing rules to examine whether they remain justified and whether they should be modified or streamlined in light of changed circumstances, including the emergence of new technologies.

In addition to the statutes and policies outlined above, the *National Technology Transfer and Advancement Act* (NTTAA) and OMB's implementing guidance to Federal agencies, *Circular No. A-119* requires Federal agencies to use[21] voluntary consensus standards[22] in their regulatory activities wherever possible and to avoid using "government-unique" standards.[23] The purpose is to discourage Federal agencies from developing their own standards where suitable voluntary consensus standards already exist. On February 11, 2014, OMB published a proposal to update A-119, and is currently seeking comments from the public on proposed revision to the Circular. The

---

[21] Circular A-119 defines "use" as the inclusion of a standard in whole, in part, or by reference in a regulation.

[22] Circular A-119 states that the following attributes define bodies that develop voluntary consensus standards: openness, balance of interests, due process, an appeals process, and consensus.

[23] Circular A-119 defines "government-unique standards" as standards developed by the government for its own uses.

proposal seeks to take account of the experience Federal agencies have gained since 1998, when Circular A-119 was originally issued. Among the proposed revisions are requirements for Federal agencies to ensure that standards in regulation are updated on a timely basis, to work with one another to reference the same version of a standard in regulation and procurements, and to increase public participation by having agencies alert the public when they are considering participation in standards development activities. These proposed changes, and others, will help guide agencies in preventing the creation of new trade barriers and avoid unnecessary regulatory differences with trading partners.

Voluntary consensus standards can often effectively achieve an agency's regulatory objectives. The NTTAA and the TAA are complementary: the NTTAA directs Federal agencies to look to voluntary consensus standards to meet their regulatory objectives, while the TAA directs them to consider using relevant international standards. *(As elaborated in Section VI, international standards are those that recognized bodies, either intergovernmental or non-governmental, develop in accordance with principles such as openness, transparency, and consensus.)*

For additional information on the laws, policies, and interagency processes through which the United States implements the TBT Agreement, see G/TBT/W/285, and G/TBT/W/315. See also the *Report on the Use of Voluntary Standards in Support of Regulation in the United States* presented to the HLRCF of the United States – European Union Transatlantic Economic Council (TEC) i October 2009. For additional information on the relationship between technical barriers to trade and GRP, see G/TBT/W/287 and USITC Working Paper No ID-24, *The Role of Good Regulatory Practice in Reducing Technical Barriers to Trade*. In 2012, APEC published two related studies. The first study, *Good Regulatory Practices in APEC Member Economies - Baseline Study* reviews the application of selected GRPs across the 21 APEC Members. The report focuses on several procedures that promote good regulatory practices particularly important to trade and investment such as accountability, consultation, efficiency, and transparency. The second study, *Supporting the TBT Agreement with Good Regulatory Practices,* explores the relationship between TBT obligations and current GRPs used around the world. These recommended GRPs demonstrate choices available to WTO Members for implementation of practices that support trade-friendly regulation and implementation of their WTO commitments.

VI. STANDARDS

Voluntary standards serve a variety of functions and their use supports world trade, for example, by promoting the connectivity and compatibility of inputs sourced in global markets. The TBT Agreement defines "standard" as: a document approved by a recognized body that provides, for common and repeated use, rules, guidelines or characteristics for products or related processes and production methods for which compliance is not mandatory.

Voluntary standards can facilitate buyer-seller transactions, spur competition[24] and innovation, increase the efficiency of production, unify markets, and promote societal goals. When used as the basis for establishing a technical requirement in a regulation, voluntary standards can help officials harness relevant technology to achieve regulatory objectives in a cost effective manner. In the United States, responsibility for developing voluntary standards rests almost exclusively, and appropriately, with the private sector, as this is where the technical know-how for sophisticated products and complex processes resides.[25]

The *TBT Agreement* seeks to minimize unnecessary obstacles to trade that can arise, for example, from specifications that favor domestic goods over imported ones, lack of transparency in the development of standards, or dominance by a region or government in standards development. To promote greater harmonization of the technical requirements that WTO Members impose, the *TBT Agreement* promotes the use of and participation in the development of international standards.

Additionally, the *TBT Agreement* requires Members to base technical regulations and conformity assessment procedures on relevant international standards, guides and recommendations, except where they would be inappropriate or ineffective in meeting a legitimate objective. The TBT Agreement affords technical regulations based on relevant international standards a rebuttable presumption that they are not unnecessary obstacles to trade under the TBT Agreement.

The TBT Agreement does not, however, designate specific standardizing bodies as "international." Instead, in the 2000 Committee Decision, the WTO TBT Committee adopted a set of six principles for developing international standards.[26]

The six principles are: (1) openness; (2) transparency; (3) impartiality and consensus; (4) relevance

---

[24] See *Standards & Competitiveness: Coordinating for Results: Removing Standards-Related Trade Barriers Through Effective Collaboration*, International Trade Administration, 2005, available at

http://www.trade.gov/td/standards/pdf%20files/Standards%20and%20Competitiveness.pdf

[25] Agriculture is a notable exception. USDA maintains several programs, such as the Agricultural Marketing Service, for the development of voluntary standards on the quality and identity of agricultural products sold in the U.S. market.

[26] Decision on Principles for the Development of International Standards, Guides and Recommendations with Relation to Articles 2, 5 and Annex 3 of the TBT Agreement are contained in document G/TBT/1/Rev.10.

and effectiveness; (5) coherence; and (6) the development dimension.

It is the policy of the U.S. Government to use the term "international standard" to refer to those standards developed in conformity with the 2000 Committee Decision principles.[27] For example, U.S. FTAs require trading partners to apply the 2000 Committee Decision principles when determining whether a relevant international standard exists. When WTO Members use international standards developed in conformity with the 2000 Committee Decision in their technical regulations, it can promote greater global regulatory alignment and reduce the adverse trade effects that regulatory divergences can create. Application of principles such as consensus, openness, and transparency when developing standards helps ensure standards are globally relevant and respond to both technical and regulatory needs. The 2000 Committee Decision also helps ensure that all interested parties, including producers and consumers that may be affected by a particular standard, can participate in developing it.

Annex 3 of the TBT Agreement contains a Code for WTO Members and non- governmental standardizing bodies to follow in preparing, adopting, and applying standards. Central government standardizing bodies must adhere to the Code.[28] WTO Members' central government standardizing bodies are required to comply with the Code, and WTO Members are required to take reasonable measures to ensure that local government bodies and non- governmental standardizing bodies conform to the Code as well. In the United States, the American National Standards Institute (ANSI) has accepted the Code on behalf of the over _200 standards developing organizations_ (SDOs) that ANSI has accredited. ANSI, a private sector body, is the coordinator of the U.S. voluntary standards system with a membership that consists of standards developers, certification bodies, industry, government, and other stakeholders. In coordination with its membership, ANSI developed and implements the _U.S. Standards Strategy._[29] _(For more information on the ANSI system, see Overview of the U.S. Standardization System.)_

ANSI accredits SDOs based on its _Essential Requirements_. These requirements largely mirror the principles contained in the 2000 Committee Decision. The _Essential Requirements_ require each SDO to maintain procedures for developing standards that ensure openness, consensus, due process, and participation by materially affected interests. ANSI also serves as the U.S. national standards body Member of the International Organization for Standardization (ISO) and the International Electrotechnical Commission (IEC). Federal agency representatives participate actively in ANSI policy forums, as well as in the technical committees of ANSI accredited SDOs, on an equal basis as other ANSI members.

OMB Circular A-119 contains guidance for Federal agencies in participating in the development of

---

[27] The U.S. experience with the _2000 Committee Decision_ is described in G/TBT/W/305.

[28] Available at http://www.wto.org/english/docs_e/legal_e/17-tbt_e.htm

[29] Available at http://www.ansi.org/standards_activities/nss/usss.aspx

voluntary standards.[30]   *Circular A-119* directs Federal agencies to use voluntary consensus standards in lieu of government unique standards except where inconsistent with law or otherwise impractical. The Circular also provides guidance for Federal agencies participating in voluntary consensus standards bodies. The Interagency Committee for Standards Policy, which NIST chairs, coordinates implementation of this guidance. More than 4,000 Federal agency officials participate in the private sector standards development activities of 497 organizations[31] to support regulatory needs, enable efficient procurement, and to help devise solutions to support emerging national priorities.   It is notable, however, that governments in some regions and countries take a nontechnical and more commanding role in standards setting than Federal agencies generally do. For example, some governments direct their national standards bodies or central government bodies to develop voluntary standards to achieve specific regulatory needs.

---

[30] Available at http://www.whitehouse.gov/omb/circulars_a119/.

[31] Source: NIST, 2008.

VII.   CONFORMITY ASSESSMENT PROCEDURES

The TBT Agreement defines "conformity assessment procedures"[32] as: "Any procedure used, directly or indirectly, to determine that relevant requirements in technical regulations or standards are fulfilled." Outside the TBT Agreement, conformity assessment procedures may also encompass a broader set of procedures, for example, good manufacturing practices that are not related to product characteristics.

Conformity assessment enables buyers, sellers, consumers, and regulators to have confidence that products sourced in domestic and foreign markets meet specific requirements.

Governments may mandate conformity assessment procedures – such as testing, sampling, and certification requirements – to ensure that the requirements they have established in standards or regulations for a product, process, system, person, or body are fulfilled. Suppliers also use conformity assessment procedures to demonstrate to their customers that their products or related processes or systems meet particular specifications.[33]

Yet, the costs and delays attributable to unnecessary, duplicative, and unclear conformity assessment requirements are frequently cited as a key concern for U.S. exporters.[34] Indeed, many specific trade concerns that the United States has raised in the WTO TBT Committee with respect to other WTO Members' measures center on difficulties associated with the Member's conformity assessment requirements. Governments can reduce or minimize such difficulties by taking into account the risks associated with a product's failure to conform to an underlying standard or requirement when choosing the type of conformity assessment procedure to apply with respect to that standard or requirement. Governments can also reduce or minimize costs associated with conformity assessment by adopting approaches that facilitate the acceptance of the results of those procedures (*e.g.,* approaches that allow products to be tested or certified in the country of export).

---

[32] Conformity assessment procedures take a variety of forms, including, for example, testing, certification, registration, inspection, accreditation, and verification. The entities that conduct these procedures are referred to as conformity assessment bodies and include such bodies as testing laboratories, certification bodies, and accreditation bodies. Testing laboratories, for example, test products to evaluate their performance or product characteristics while certification bodies certify that products conform to specific standards or requirements. Accreditation bodies, for example, evaluate the competency of testing and certification bodies and verify that they comply with specific standards or requirements.

[33] For an introduction to conformity assessment, see Breitenberg, Maureen, *The ABC's of the U.S. Conformity Assessment System,* NIST, 1997

[34] See Johnson, Christopher, *Technical Barriers to Trade: Reducing the Impact of Conformity Assessment Measures,* U.S. International Trade Commission Working Paper, 2008

The WTO TBT Committee's list of approaches that facilitate this acceptance is contained in G/TBT/1/Rev.11.

In the United States, the NTTAA directs NIST to coordinate the conformity assessment activities of Federal, State, and local entities with private sector technical standards activities and conformity assessment activities. The goal is to eliminate any unnecessary duplication of these activities. Pursuant to this statutory directive, NIST published a notice in the *Federal Register* in 2000 providing *Guidance to Federal Agencies on Conformity Assessment*.[35] This notice calls for Federal agencies to provide sound rationales, seek public comments, look to the results of other government and private sector organizations, and use international guides and standards when incorporating conformity assessment procedures in their regulations and procurement processes. The conformity assessment standards and guides published by ISO and IEC are known as the "CASCO toolbox, which are the international standards and guides agencies are encouraged to use."[36]

In addition to NIST's efforts to inform and guide Federal agencies in adopting and applying conformity assessment procedures, Federal agencies and private sector organizations can look to guidance in ANSI's *National Conformity Assessment Principles for the United States*.[37] OMB's proposal to update *Circular A-119* also contains guidance to Federal agencies with respect to conformity assessment. The TBT Agreement, NIST's guidance, ANSI's principles, and OMB's proposal to update Circular A-119 all emphasize the importance of the development and use of international conformity assessment standards and participation in international accreditation systems in facilitating international trade.

Participation and use of international systems of conformity assessment strengthens these international systems and produces global benefits. For example, international systems for accreditation play a vital role in allowing products to be tested and certified at sites that are convenient to production facilities and reducing duplicative testing and certification requirements. International systems for accreditation enable this by establishing procedures and criteria that accreditation bodies participating in the system agree to apply when accrediting testing, certification, or other conformity assessment bodies. Accreditations issued by such entities can, in appropriate circumstances, provide governments, as well as suppliers, assurances that a body – regardless of its location – is competent to test and certify products for relevant markets.

Examples of international accreditation systems include the International Laboratory Accreditation Cooperation (ILAC) and the International Accreditation Forum (IAF). ILAC and IAF have established voluntary MRAs. Under these MRAs, accreditation bodies agree to adhere to

---

[35] http://gsi.nist.gov/global/docs/FR_FedGuidanceCA.pdf

[36] ISO/CASCO is the standards development and policy committee on conformity assessment of ISO.

[37] http://publicaa.ansi.org/sites/apdl/Documents/News%20and%20Publications/Brochures/NCAP%20second%20edition.pdf

international standards and other procedures and criteria when accrediting testing and certification bodies and subject themselves to a system of peer to peer review to ensure that they continue to meet MRA requirements. Accreditation bodies that participate in these mutual recognition arrangements are predominately private sector entities in the United States. Increasingly, Federal agencies, such as the Consumer Product Safety Commission and the Nuclear Regulatory Commission, are using international systems such as ILAC in support of their conformity assessment requirements.

VIII. U.S. PROCESSES FOR IDENTIFYING STANDARDS-RELATED TRADE BARRIERSAND DETERMINING HOW TO ADDRESS THEM

The United States maintains rigorous, interagency processes and mechanisms for identifying, reviewing, analyzing, and addressing foreign government standards-related measures that act, or may act, as barriers to U.S. trade. USTR coordinates these processes and mechanisms through the TPSC and, more specifically, its specialized TBT subgroup, the TPSC Subcommittee on Technical Barriers to Trade (TPSC Subcommittee).

The TPSC Subcommittee, comprising representatives from Federal agencies and other agencies with an interest in foreign standards-related measures, meets formally at least three times a year, but maintains an ongoing process of informal consultation and coordination on standards-related issues as they arise. Representatives of the TPSC Subcommittee include officials from the U.S. Departments of Agriculture, Commerce, and State – as well as officials from OMB and Federal agencies, such as the U.S. Food and Drug Administration and the U.S. Environmental Protection Agency. The U.S. Departments of Commerce and Agriculture serve as the primary conduits for communicating information between U.S. industry and agriculture export interests, respectively, and the TPSC Subcommittee.

Information for the TPSC Subcommittee on foreign standards-related measures is collected and evaluated on a day to day basis through a variety of government channels including: the U.S. TBT Inquiry Point and Notification Authority (U.S. TBT Inquiry Point) at NIST, the Trade Compliance Center (TCC), the Office of Standards Liaison, and the U.S. Commercial Service (UCS) in the U.S. Department of Commerce; the Foreign Agricultural Service (FAS) and its Office of Agreements and Scientific Affairs (OASA) in the U.S. Department of Agriculture and its officers in U.S. embassies abroad; the U.S. State Department's economic officers in U.S embassies abroad; and USTR. U.S. Government outreach and consultations with U.S. stakeholders generates much of the information supplied through these channels, which are further described below.

To disseminate information to U.S. stakeholders on proposed foreign notifications of standards-related measures, the U.S. Inquiry Point operates a web based service, Notify U.S., which automatically notifies registered stakeholders of measures proposed and adopted by other WTO Members in sectors of interest.[38] These notifications alert U.S. firms and other interested

---

[38] Available at https://tsapps.nist.gov/notifyus/data/index/index.cfm

stakeholders of their opportunity to comment on proposed foreign measures that may have an impact on their exports. U.S. stakeholders may provide their comments directly to the WTO Member concerned, if its domestic processes so provide, or through the U.S. Inquiry Point, which works with relevant Federal agencies to review, compile and submit comments to the WTO Member. U.S. stakeholders, by providing comments through the U.S. Inquiry Point, alert Federal agencies to their concerns and enable advocacy by Federal agencies on their behalf.

In 2013, the U.S. TBT Inquiry Point distributed 2,139 WTO TBT notifications to registered stakeholders, including 103 U.S. notifications. The U.S. TBT Inquiry Point processed 266 requests for information on standards and technical regulations and fulfilled 431 requests for full text documents associated with TBT notifications. The U.S. TBT Inquiry Point distributed 196 U.S. Government and industry comments to other WTO Members and circulated 34 WTO Member comments on U.S. measures, as well as 54 WTO Member replies to U.S. comments, to relevant Federal agencies. U.S. stakeholders monitor notifications of new or revised measures of other WTO Members in sectors of interest through Notify U.S. (which added more than 450 new subscribers in 2013), and contact U.S. officials through the government channels listed above to obtain further information, to contribute to the submission of U.S. comments, and to coordinate follow up actions. The U.S TBT Inquiry Point hosted or participated in training for nine U.S. and foreign visiting delegations interested in learning how a WTO inquiry point operates.

During 2013, the U.S. Department of Commerce's International Trade Administration consolidated its business divisions, reducing them from four to three units to better align key functions to support U.S. businesses and their workers. The new units are Enforcement and Compliance (E&C), Global Markets (GM), and Industry and Analysis (I&A), which include experts on enforcement of U.S. trade laws and compliance with trade agreements, country and regional issues, and industry issues, respectively. The Office of Trade Agreements Negotiations and Compliance (TANC) in E&C coordinates TBT related work at the U.S. Department of Commerce, including representing the U.S. Department of Commerce on interagency teams dealing with TBT and regulatory coherence issues and serving as the U.S. Department of Commerce member of the U.S. delegation to the WTO TBT Committee. TANC also leads the Trade Agreements Compliance (TAC) Program, which supports the enforcement of over 250 international trade agreements to which the United States is a party. The GM unit works with U.S. companies to help them expand market access opportunities abroad. GM has specialists at the U.S. Department of Commerce's headquarters, as well as in 100 U.S. cities and in 73 countries around the world, including Standards Attachés in four key markets (Mexico, Brazil, the EU and China) to provide on the ground assistance for U.S. companies with standards-related trade issues. The I&A unit, including the new Office of Standards and Investment Policy focuses on industry or sector specific negotiations, standards development, and good regulatory practice and capacity building in APEC and the Association of Southeast Asian Nations (ASEAN), among other fora. It also shares with USTR primary responsibility for administering the Industry Trade Advisory Committee on Standards and Technical Trade Barriers.

Through the TAC Program, the U.S. Department of Commerce supports the enforcement prong of the NEI by coordinating efforts and resources within the Department to systematically monitor, investigate, and help ensure foreign governments' compliance with trade agreements to which the United States is a party. The TAC Program includes an online trade complaint hotline at www.export.gov/tcc, where exporters can report and obtain assistance in overcoming foreign trade barriers. As part of the TAC Program, the U.S. Department of Commerce assembles teams of specialists to investigate market access problems, including those involving standards-related measures, as well as to develop strategies to address them. Compliance team's work with affected companies or industries to establish objectives and to craft and implement compliance action plans to achieve or improve market access.

In addition, the U.S. Department of Commerce regularly provides input to the TPSC and TPSC Subcommittee based on the information on the specific trade concerns that it collects and analyzes through the TAC Program. This informs the TPSC's development of the appropriate U.S. position in the various multilateral and bilateral forums for addressing standards-related measures. Compliance officers also provide on the ground assistance at U.S. embassies in China, India, El Salvador, and at the U.S. Mission to the European Union in Brussels. Free, online tools include the texts of more than 250 non-agricultural trade agreements plus a checklist of the kinds of trade barriers that the TAC Program can help exporters overcome.

The Department of Agriculture's Foreign Agricultural Service (FAS) provides a conduit for queries and comments on foreign standards-related measures in the agricultural sector. The Office of Agreements and Scientific Affairs (OASA) monitors developments in relevant export markets, provides information on foreign standards-related measures through a range of publications, disseminates TBT notifications from foreign governments to interested parties, and provides translation services on key export market requirements. OASA works cooperatively with U.S. industry, as well as with technical specialists in its overseas offices and Federal agencies, to develop comments and positions on specific foreign standards- related measures. As a way to streamline processes and make information more accessible for U.S. agricultural exporters, OASA established a trade facilitation desk. The one stop service helps U.S. exporters navigate the complexities of the export process and makes it easier for them to access opportunities in every corner of the world. The trade facilitation desk assists U.S. exporters to obtain information on export certification, registration, and the documentation requirements for international trade, as well as alert the U.S. Department of Agriculture (USDA) when U.S. food and agriculture shipments are detained or refused. In addition, FAS's overseas offices maintain country specific reporting and alerts that highlight foreign commodity specific import requirements. These officers assist with detained shipments and help to identify innovative solutions to keep trade flowing. Finally, FAS also participates in numerous relevant international organizations, such as Codex Alimentarius, to proactively address agriculture-related trade concerns arising from foreign standards-related measures.

In addition to these government channels, the TPSC Subcommittee receives information from the Industry and Agriculture Trade Advisory Committees (ITACs and ATACs, respectively). The ITACs and the ATACs help identify trade barriers and provide assessments regarding the practical realities that producers face in complying with technical regulations and conformity assessment procedures. USTR and U.S. Department of Commerce officials meet at least quarterly with the ITAC on Standards and Technical Trade Barriers (ITAC 16), which is composed of cleared advisors from manufacturers, trade associations, standards developers, and conformity assessment bodies.[39]

In 2013, the ITAC 16 met six times. USTR also meets with other ITACs and advisory committees to receive advice on TBT issues affecting specific industry sectors, such as steel, chemicals, automobiles, processed foods, and textiles, or specific regulatory areas, such as labor and the environment. In 2013, the six Technical Advisory Committees for Trade in Agriculture (ATACs) met 13 times with U.S. Department of Agriculture and USTR officials to provide advice on TBT issues affecting specific agricultural sectors and their related products such as animals; fruits and vegetables; grains, feed and oilseeds; processed food products; and sweeteners, tobacco, cotton and peanuts.

In developing the U.S. position on any foreign standards-related measure, the TPSC Subcommittee takes into account how the United States regulates the same or similar products. Regulatory agency officials on the TBT TPSC Subcommittee also provide important information on the technical and scientific aspects of particular foreign standards-related measures, as well as insights on cooperative efforts through international organizations that may be relevant to the issue. The TPSC Subcommittee factors the views that regulatory agencies express into the positions that the United States takes in multilateral, regional, and bilateral trade discussions regarding standards-related measures. Particularly in the area of emerging technologies where standards-related activities are nascent, the technical, scientific, and policy advice that regulatory agencies provide is critical in formulating U.S. views.

Engagement in Voluntary Standards Activities

In the United States, standards development is led by the private sector and highly informed by market needs. However, in limited circumstances, in areas relevant to their agency objectives, Federal agencies also actively engage, or play a convening role in standards development. In January 2012, *Principles for Federal Engagement in Standards Activities to Address National Priorities*[40] were sent by USTR, OMB, and Office of Science and Technology Policy (OSTP) to agencies to clarify principles guiding Federal agencies' engagement in standards activities. The memorandum emphasizes the strengths of the U.S. standards model of private sector leadership but notes that where a national priority has been identified in statute, regulation, or Administration policy, active engagement or a convening role by the Federal Government may be needed to accelerate standards development and implementation to spur technological advances, promote market based innovation, and encourage more competitive market outcomes. The memorandum

---

[39] See http://www.ustr.gov/Who_We_Are/List_of_USTR_Advisory_Committees.html.

[40] Available at http://www.whitehouse.gov/sites/default/files/omb/memoranda/2012/m-12-08.pdf

establishes five "fundamental strategic objectives" for Federal Government engagement in standards activities:

- produce timely, effective standards and efficient conformity assessment schemes that are essential to addressing an identified need;

- achieve cost-efficient, timely, and effective solutions to legitimate regulatory, procurement, and policy objectives;

- promote standards and standardization systems that promote and sustain innovation and foster competition;

- enhance U.S. growth and competitiveness and ensure non-discrimination, consistent with international obligations; and

- facilitate international trade and avoid the creation of unnecessary obstacles to trade.

Circular A-119 also addresses Federal agencies' participation in standards development.

IX. U.S. ENGAGEMENT ON STANDARDS-RELATED MEASURES IN INTERNATIONAL, REGIONAL, AND BILATERAL FORA

Overview of U.S. Engagement on Standards-Related Measures

The United States pursues a broad agenda and active engagement with foreign governments to prevent unnecessary obstacles to trade and to resolve specific trade concerns arising from standards-related measures. As noted above, the WTO TBT Committee is the principal multilateral forum for engagement on trade issues relating to standards-related measures. The mechanisms for cooperation on these measures in U.S. FTAs also play a vital role in facilitating U.S. efforts to prevent and resolve standards-related trade concerns. In addition, U.S. agencies seek to prevent potential standards-related trade barriers from emerging by engaging in multilateral, regional, and bilateral cooperative activities, information exchanges, technical assistance, and negotiations on specific agreements. These efforts are aimed at helping other governments design effective and well-conceived standards-related measures, with the goal of producing better regulatory outcomes and facilitating trade.

U.S. Government cooperative efforts and information exchanges with other countries can assist firms in complying with standards-related measures. As producers increase their participation in global supply chains, they need a better understanding of various countries' technical requirements, including the United States, and strategies to meet those requirements consistently. Cooperative activities can also serve to prevent localized high profile incidents of the type that can disrupt trade across all markets and damage both producer reputations and consumer confidence. Close coordination among trade, regulatory, and standards officials with highly specialized technical expertise among other things is required in order to carry out cooperation and information exchange initiatives that successfully meet these objectives.

The United States provides bilateral technical assistance and capacity building to developing countries on standards-related activities through the U.S. Agency for International Development (USAID), the U.S. Trade and Development Agency, the U.S. Department of Commerce's Commercial Law Development Program (CLDP) and Market Development Cooperator Program, and NIST's Standards in Trade Program. USDA's FAS also provides technical assistance on standards-related food trade. These agencies have broader missions and generally provide standards-related capacity building assistance as a component of a specific project or mission.

To reduce the negative impact on trade from divergences in technical requirements across markets, the United States negotiates bilateral, regional, and multilateral MRAs with U.S. trading partners. These agreements establish procedures for each party to accept the results of conformity assessment procedures for specified products carried out in the other party's territory or to accept the other government's technical specifications for those products as sufficient to meet its own requirements. MRAs with trading partners that have a regulatory approach compatible with that of the United States and a similar level of technical capacity can help facilitate trade in select sectors where trade flows are significant and technical requirements can be complex, such as in the telecommunication equipment sector.

NIST maintains a complete inventory of the government to government MRAs to which the United States is a party.[41] It also maintains a listing of the accreditation requirements for conformity assessment bodies under each of these MRAs and a list of conformity assessment bodies that NIST has designated pursuant to each MRA as competent to perform tests or certify products to ensure they conform to the other MRA party's technical requirements. The Federal Communications Commission website provides useful background information on U.S. MRAs in the telecommunications sector and examples of how they work.[42]

The United States also seeks to reduce foreign technical barriers to trade by concluding equivalency arrangements with other governments. The United States has now exchanged three organic equivalency arrangements. The first organic equivalency arrangement concluded with Canada in 2009, the second with the EU in 2012, and the third with Japan in 2013.

(U.S. engagement on standards-related measures in various international and regional fora is detailed below. U.S. bilateral engagement with its trading partners on standards-related measures is detailed in individual Country Specific Reports in Section XI.)

WTO TBT Committee and Related Engagement

As noted above, the U.S. Government actively seeks to prevent and eliminate unnecessary technical barriers to trade through the focused WTO Member driven agenda of the WTO TBT Committee. The WTO TBT Committee dedicates a significant portion of each of its three annual meetings to affording Members the opportunity to raise specific trade concerns on measures that other Members have proposed or adopted. WTO Members may also use Committee sessions to share experiences, case studies, or concerns relating to cross cutting issues regarding how Members are implementing the TBT Agreement. The WTO TBT Committee often holds workshops or other events on special topics alongside its formal meetings. On the margins of each meeting, Members engage in informal bilateral and plurilateral meetings to clarify and resolve specific trade concerns and to discuss how to resolve other issues of mutual interest.

Specific Trade Concerns

In 2013, the United States raised specific trade concerns regarding on average 20 to 30 foreign TBT measures at each WTO TBT Committee meeting and in the informal meetings it held with

---

[41] Available at http://gsi.nist.gov/global/index.cfm/L1-4/L2-16.

[42] Available at http://transition.fcc.gov/oet/ea/mra/

individual or groups of WTO Members. *(The details and status of many of the specific trade concerns that the United States raised in, and on the margins of, the WTO TBT Committee sessions are described in Section XI of this report. As elaborated in Section XI, U.S. interventions in the TBT Committee, and on its margins, have helped resolve a number of standards-related concerns affecting U.S. trade.)* The Committee's annual review of its activities is contained in G/TBT/29, which includes a thumbnail description of the specific trade concerns that WTO Members raised and identifies the Members that raised them.

Systemic Issues

The TBT Agreement calls for the WTO TBT Committee to review the implementation and operation of the Agreement every three years. These triennial reviews provide an important opportunity for WTO Members to clarify particular provisions of the Agreement. Triennial reviews have resulted in a significant body of agreed recommendations and decisions, contained in G/TBT/1/Rev.11, which are intended to strengthen and improve the operation of the TBT Agreement. Each triennial review also results in a report on the systemic issues the Committee discussed, along with a work plan to explore ways in which WTO Members can more effectively implement their TBT obligations.

In November 2011, the WTO TBT Committee initiated its Sixth Triennial Review of the Operation and Implementation of the Agreement on Technical Barriers to Trade under Article 15.4. In the review, which concluded in November 2012, the Committee agreed to exchanges of information on (1) voluntary mechanisms and related principles of Good Regulatory Practices to guide Members in efficient and effective implementation of the TBT Agreement; (2) approaches to, recognition of, and use of international standards for conformity assessment; (3) implementation of the Code of Good Practice by local governments and non-governmental bodies; and (4) the six principles of international standards development set out in the 2000 Committee Decision, with particular focus on the development dimension and transparency.

In 2013, with a view to implementing the goals of the 6th Triennial Review, the WTO TBT Committee held special thematic sessions on Good Regulatory Practices, Standards Development, Special and Differential Treatment, Capacity Building and Operations of the WTO Inquiry Points.

Technical Assistance and Capacity Building

Standards Alliance

The United States also launched a new assistance facility called the "Standards Alliance" in November 2012 to help build capacity among developing countries to implement the TBT Agreement. The Standards Alliance will help developing countries strengthen implementation of the TBT Agreement, including by helping them to improve their notification practices and domestic practices related to adopting relevant international standards and to clarify and streamline their regulatory processes for products. This program aims to reduce the costs and bureaucratic hurdles

U.S. exporters face in foreign markets, and increase the competitiveness of American products, particularly in developing markets.

In May 2013, USAID and ANSI entered into a partnership that will coordinate private sector subject matter experts from ANSI member organizations to deliver training and facilitate technical exchanges with interested Standards Alliance countries.

The project will include activities in up to ten markets representing a variety of geographical regions and levels of economic development. In consultation with U.S. Government and private sector experts, ANSI reviewed the applications received with consideration of bilateral trade opportunities, available private sector expertise, demonstrated commitment and readiness for assistance, and potential development impact. Participating countries or regions for the first year will include: Central America (CAFTA-DR, Panama), Colombia, East African Community, Indonesia, Middle East and North Africa, Peru, Southern Africa Development Community, developing ASEAN members, and Yemen.

Standards Alliance programming accomplishments in 2013 include a bilateral workshop on Good Regulatory Practices with Indonesia in June 2013, and a series of programs with Peru held between July and September 2013 on standards development, conformity assessment, good regulatory practices, and implementation of the WTO Agreement on Technical Barriers to Trade, conducted in both in Peru and the United States.

Total Economic Engagement Program

The U.S. Department of Commerce's Total Economic Engagement (TEE) Program provides technical assistance and capacity building to developing countries to advance a more collaborative and open standardization and regulatory process, to increase developing country regulators' exposure to the views of the private sector, and to foster greater regulatory alignment and convergence. TEE works with foreign governments, trade associations, and standards setting bodies on key public-private partnerships.

For example, in 2013 the TEE program supported regional workshops in the United Arab Emirates and Egypt to address automotive standards concerns in the Middle East and North Africa region. Regulators from the U.S. National Highway Traffic Safety Administration, and the U.S. Federal Motor Carrier Safety Administration, along with automotive industry associations and automobile makers, engaged in technical exchanges with regulators and national standards body representatives from a number of economies on vehicle safety and emissions standards and regulatory requirements currently being updated.

There was also ongoing work with the Russian Federation on implementation of Russia's WTO commitments that included a TBT and standards best practices exchange seminar aimed at preventing technical barriers to trade.

In 2013, the TEE also supported an information exchange between Brazil's medical device regulatory agency (ANVISA), the U.S. Food and Drug Administration and industry on international medical device regulatory harmonization efforts and best practices in medical device regulation.

U.S. Department of Commerce Commercial Law Development Program

In 2013, the CLDP program has been engaged in capacity building to assist countries in implementing the obligations of the WTO Agreement on Technical Barriers to Trade. The CLDP programming included orientation visits of Iraqi officials to the United States in April 2013 and a capacity building program on implementation of the WTO Agreement on Technical Barriers to Trade for several of the Middle East and Northern African trading partners in cooperation with the Gulf Standards Organization in May 2013. Because of CLDP capacity building efforts, Morocco, Jordan and Yemen joined the Standards Alliance program in 2013.

Association of Southeast Asian Nations

The Association of Southeast Asian Nations (ASEAN) was established as a regional organization in 1967 to accelerate economic growth, promote regional peace and stability, and enhance cooperation on economic, social, cultural, technical, and educational matters among Southeast Asian countries. Member states include Brunei Darussalam, Cambodia, Indonesia, Laos, Malaysia, Myanmar, Singapore, Thailand, Vietnam, and the Philippines.

The United States supports deepening commercial engagement with ASEAN under the United States-ASEAN Expanded Economic Engagement (E3) Initiative, under the ASEAN-U.S. Trade and Investment Framework Arrangement. The E3 Initiative is intended to help lay the groundwork for ASEAN countries to pursue high-standard trade agreements, such as the TPP, and includes an element of cooperation on standards development and practices.

The U.S Department of Commerce carries out the standards cooperation work under the ASEAN Consultative Committee on Standards and Quality (ACCSQ), and is supported by funding from USAID. The focus is on sectors that appear on both ASEAN's list of 12 Priority Sectors and in the U.S. National Export Strategy with the objective of encouraging good regulatory practices and the use of international standards, and increasing ASEAN participation in international regulatory cooperation activities to facilitate trade and reduce nontariff barriers. Priority sectors include medical devices, building products, dietary supplements, food safety, green chemistry, electrical and electronic goods, and information and communications technology (ICT) products. This work helps ensure that U.S. products have access to the ASEAN regional market.

In 2013, activities included programs on medical device regulatory capacity building, green building codes and building information modeling to facilitate green commercial construction, food incident management and building SME capacity in food safety standards, and the application of "green chemistry" to specific industries. Food safety and green building activities are carried out jointly with the APEC Sub-Committee on Standards and Conformance (SCSC) and Food Safety Cooperation Forum (FSCF).

Asia Pacific Economic Cooperation

APEC is the Asia Pacific region's premier inter-governmental economic organization. Its core mission is to strengthen regional economic integration by addressing barriers to trade and investment. APEC's 21 Member economies comprise nearly half the world's population and more than half of the global economy. These Member economies account for 55 percent of global GDP, purchase 58 percent of U.S. goods exports, and comprise a market of 2.7 billion customers. In fact, 7 of the top 15 trade partners of the United States are Members of APEC. In 2013, Indonesia hosted APEC and focused on three areas: attainment of the Bogor Goals, the achievement of sustainable growth with equity, and the promotion of connectivity.

Underscoring its commitment to engage the Asia Pacific region on a range of economic and other issues and support APEC's goal of regional integration, the U.S. Government launched the United States-APEC Technical Assistance to Advance Regional Integration (US-ATAARI) program in November 2013. The program will be a five year project co-managed by USAID Regional Development Mission for Asia and USAID's Washington based Office of Trade and Regulatory Reform within the Bureau for Economic Growth, Education, and Environment with funding and strategic direction from the U.S. Department of State's Office of Economic Policy within the Bureau of East Asian and Pacific Affairs. The funds are currently anticipated to be $27.5 million for the life of the project.

US-ATAARI builds upon past assistance provided to APEC economies by the U.S. Government by delivering targeted technical assistance, ranging from policy studies and assessments to capacity building, training and expert advice on integration, trade liberalization and institutional management. The project is designed to support regional economic integration within the APEC region via activities that support ongoing work within each of APEC's three pillars (trade and investment liberalization; business facilitation; and economic and technical cooperation), and that align with U.S. foreign policy priorities.

Work on standards related measures takes place in the SCSC where the United States continues to play a leadership role in encouraging the SCSC to focus on good regulatory practice in specific sectors and initiating early regional engagement in emerging technology areas so that standards and conformity assessment measures do not become unnecessary obstacles to trade. The United States currently leads three multiyear projects in the SCSC on food, green building and wine, and will continue work on the energy efficiency of ICT products with a new project in 2014.

Electric Vehicles Standards

The United States is working with other APEC economies that may choose to regulate electric vehicles. This initiative is aimed at promoting the production and use of electric vehicles by preventing economies from developing unique regulatory approaches and creating unnecessary regulatory divergences. To prepare for a dialogue on this topic in May 2014 in Qingdao, China, the United States is drafting two analytical pieces: (1) a literature review on existing international standards for electric vehicles; and (2) a study on how APEC economies are currently regulating in this space. We are working with China, Japan, and other interested APEC economies to produce recommendations for Leaders to consider in November on promoting alignment of international electric vehicle standards.

Good Regulatory Practice

APEC economies recognized the importance of GRPs, addressing unnecessary technical barriers to trade, and advancing regulatory convergence and coherence. In June 2013, Indonesia hosted the 7th Conference on Good Regulatory Practice in Medan, Indonesia. The conference assessed progress made by economies towards implementing the 2011 APEC Leaders' commitment to strengthen the implementation of GRPs by ensuring internal coordination of rulemaking, assessing the impact of regulations, and conducting public consultations and highlighted the role that standards and conformity assessment play in supporting GRPs. Participants supported efforts in APEC to improve transparency through mechanisms that develop single websites for regulatory information, encouraged APEC economies to engage in retrospective review of regulations, and called for capacity building and education efforts with regulators, government officials, and industry to build support and understanding of GRP.

The United States also funded a study, "Good Regulatory Practices for Conformity Assessment in APEC Member Economies." This study examined the conformity assessment procedures in Member economies and how they incorporate GRPs with respect to conformity assessment and ensure protection of health, safety, and the environment without creating unnecessary barriers to trade. The study gave particular focus to the electrical installations, photovoltaic, and medical devices/pacemakers sectors. APEC also completed a progress report on its work to update the "Baseline Study of Good Regulatory Practices in APEC Member Economies," scheduled to be fully completed by the Third Senior Officials' Meeting (SOM 3) in 2015.

The United States also hosted a workshop in Washington, D.C., on November 12 to 15, 2013 on the benefits and use of electronic rulemaking, which help advance the 2014 goals of improving public consultations in the Internet era.

In 2014, we are seeking to have APEC Leaders commit to undertaking a series of actions by 2020 on improving public consultations on proposed regulations through information technology, making APEC a global leader in this area. We are also seeking Leaders' establishment of a capacity building plan to assist economies' implementation of these commitments. To support this effort, the United States is developing a study on stakeholder and regulator experiences with using information technology in their public consultations.

Green Buildings

Green buildings provide opportunities for U.S. companies to export a wide range of green products in which they have a competitive advantage, such as products related to plumbing, lighting, flooring, HVAC systems, and fixtures. The United States launched work on green building standards, codes and rating systems in 2011, building on the direction from Leaders and Ministers to support the transition towards low carbon economies in the Asia Pacific region. Green building is a new technology area where there is an opportunity to ensure that the standards and conformity assessment requirements that underpin trade in these technologies do not create unnecessary trade barriers for U.S. industry. Greening the commercial building sector can also yield significant energy savings since the commercial building sector accounts for approximately 40 percent of energy usage in most industrialized economies.

Work in 2013 focused on building codes and building information modeling (BIM) as the United States began to implement activities under a new multiyear project on green building. In March 2013, Peru and the United States organized a workshop on green codes in Lima, Peru, which was followed by the completion of a comprehensive study: *APEC Building Codes, Regulations and Standards: Minimum, Mandatory and Green*. In June 2013, a second workshop explored how BIM can be utilized to drive green building by delivering concrete benefits in the planning, design, construction and operation of buildings; economies can assess progress in BIM utilization using an *APEC BIM Quick Start Guide*. The United States is working together with the ASEAN ACCSQ on the green building project.

In 2014, work on green buildings will continue in APEC. The 2014 APEC Conference on Standards and Conformance for Green Technologies, scheduled to be held in Beijing, China in August will include sessions on green codes and BIM.

Wine Regulatory Forum

The SCSC created a Wine Regulatory Forum (WRF) in 2008 to promote trade facilitating regulation of wine. Regulatory coherence in the APEC region is a priority because wine trade has grown dramatically in importance for developing and exporting economies. The value of this trade increased from $1.1 billion in 2000 to $3.6 billion in 2010, however, a growing number of unnecessary nontariff barriers estimated to cost businesses (primarily SMEs) approximately $1 billion a year, impedes trade in wine.

In 2011 and 2012, APEC WRF meetings focused on promoting regulator dialogue and cooperation, exchanging current practices, educating economies on wine's low risk profile, and building confidence in each country's regulatory regime. In 2013 the United States, through a multiyear project, continued to build on the outcomes of those meetings by assisting developing economies to implement specific, measurable good regulatory practices with respect to wine regulation. Through active participation in the project, these economies will gain improved assurance of the safety of imported wine. A reduction in unnecessary impediments to trade, such as redundant export certificate requirements, and a better understanding of foreign regulatory regimes and wine science, will lead to increased opportunities for developing economy wine exports. The first activity under the project occurred in November 2013 when the WRF held a technical meeting in Washington in conjunction with the World Wine Trade Group meeting. In September 2014, The WRF will meet again in Beijing, China in conjunction with the Food Safety Cooperation Forum to discuss improving regulation acceptance of export certificates and to more closely align practices on Maximum Residue Limits (MRLs) for pesticides.

The SCSC multiyear projects on wine and food safety share a connection in that the FSCF is working on a regulatory roadmap for pesticide MRLs that has identified wine grape MRLs as a pilot area. Wine regulators are engaged in the FSCF working group on MRLs.

ICT Energy Efficiency

The SCSC has already completed two workshops on ICT energy efficiency since 2011. APEC recently awarded funding for a new U.S. led project to continue advancing regional alignment to IEC standards and conformity assessment procedures for laptops and personal computers, and an ICT Energy Efficiency Regulators Forum has been created so APEC economies can regularly discuss this topic. This work has the strong support of the U.S. ICT industry. Plans call for the ICT workshop to be held during SOM 3 in Beijing, China in August 2014 as part of the APEC Conference on Standards and Conformance for Green Technologies.

Trans-Pacific Partnership

In November 2009, President Obama announced that the United States would participate in negotiations to conclude a comprehensive Asia Pacific trade agreement, the Trans-Pacific Partnership (TPP) Agreement. Through the TPP, the United States seeks to advance U.S. trade and investment opportunities in the Asia Pacific by negotiating an ambitious, 21st century regional trade agreement. In addition to the United States, the TPP negotiations currently include: Australia, Brunei Darussalam, Canada, Chile, Japan, Malaysia, Mexico, New Zealand, Peru, Singapore, and Vietnam. The twelve countries have made considerable progress toward concluding the negotiations, including on standards-related issues, on which the United States is seeking to establish rules and disciplines for standards-related measures that reduce or eliminate unwarranted barriers to trade.

In 2013, the TPP Technical Barriers to Trade negotiating group made substantial progress toward conclusion of the TBT chapter and several sector specific annexes. The TPP TBT Chapter will build on the WTO TBT Agreement and include obligations on regulatory transparency, the use of GRPs, the acceptance of the results of conformity assessment procedures carried out in TPP countries, and international standards. It will also set out a framework for addressing trade concerns and for advancing cooperative activities on standards-related measures.

The TPP also will have sector specific annexes including obligations regarding the development and implementation of standards-related measures to address unnecessary barriers to trade in cosmetics, pharmaceuticals, medical devices, information and ICT, wine and spirits, organics, footwear and food formulas.

Transatlantic Trade and Investment Partnership

On June 17, 2013 President Obama and EU leaders launched negotiations on a comprehensive trade and investment agreement, the Transatlantic Trade and Investment Partnership (T-TIP), with the objective of increasing jobs, economic growth and competitiveness on both sides of the Atlantic. Given that T-TIP's potential benefits stem in large part from the parties' ability to significantly reduce or eliminate nontariff barriers, addressing nontariff barriers in the form of regulatory restrictions that impose significant costs, create unnecessary barriers, reduce efficiency in the transatlantic market, and limit the capacity of U.S. and EU firms to innovate and compete in global markets, is a key aspect of achieving the more integrated transatlantic marketplace envisaged by TTIP. Thus, in the negotiations the United States seeks to reduce such barriers and prevent future ones, while ensuring our continued ability to regulate to achieve health, safety, environmental and other legitimate regulatory objectives.

In order to deliver an agreement that will be a driver of job creation, economic growth and competitiveness, the United States is seeking with respect to nontariff barriers and regulatory issues to establish new rules and obligations in T-TIP to strengthen the ability of U.S. and EU firms to compete globally, as well as support the multilateral trading system through approaches consistent with most favored nation and national treatment. The U.S. view is that such ambitious outcomes can be achieved if they are based on regulatory approaches that have long been observed to support and enable successful economic growth, market integration and removal of trade barriers, such as policies promoting transparency and accountability, innovation, open markets and competition. For the United States, a natural point of departure is to draw from, build on, and move beyond the broad array of current commitments, guiding principles and good practices agreed over the past twenty years through the WTO, the OECD and other organizations, as well as in United States-European Union cooperation efforts on trade and regulatory issues.

The negotiations on regulatory issues are proceeding on the basis of the five elements on regulatory issues and nontariff barriers contained in the final report of the United States-European Union High-Level Working Group (HLWG, issued on February 11, 2013:

- An ambitious "SPS-plus" chapter, including establishment of an ongoing mechanism for improved dialogue and cooperation on addressing bilateral sanitary and phytosanitary (SPS) issues. The negotiations will build upon the key principles of the *SPS Agreement*, including the requirements that each side's SPS measures be based on science and on international standards or scientific risk assessments, applied only to the extent necessary to protect human, animal, or plant life or health, and developed in a transparent manner, without undue delay.

- An ambitious "TBT-plus" chapter, building on horizontal disciplines in the *TBT Agreement*, including establishment of an ongoing mechanism for improved dialogue and cooperation for addressing bilateral TBT issues. The objectives of the chapter are to yield greater openness, transparency, and convergence in regulatory approaches and requirements and related standards development processes, as well as, *inter alia*, to reduce redundant and burdensome testing and certification requirements, promote confidence in our respective conformity assessment bodies, and enhance cooperation on conformity assessment and standardization issues globally.

- Cross cutting disciplines on regulatory coherence and transparency for the development and implementation of efficient, cost effective, and more compatible regulations for goods and services, including early consultations on significant regulations, use of impact assessments, periodic review of existing regulatory measures, and application of good regulatory practices.

- Provisions or annexes containing additional commitments or steps aimed at promoting regulatory compatibility in specific, mutually agreed goods and services sectors, with the objective of reducing costs stemming from regulatory differences in specific sectors, including consideration of approaches relating to regulatory harmonization, equivalence, or mutual recognition, where appropriate.

- A framework for identifying opportunities for and guiding future regulatory cooperation, including provisions that provide an institutional basis for future progress.

All but the SPS-plus element are related to TBT. The U.S. negotiating objectives in these five areas are based on the domestic consultation procedures undertaken with Congress, the Trade Policy Staff Committee (TPSC), and the public. The TPSC received over 370 submissions from a range of interests, many pertaining to the regulatory area. The submissions emphasized the following concerns on standards and regulatory issues:

- U.S. persons are not able to participate directly and effectively in the development of regulations, standards and conformity assessment procedures in the EU. In particular, some institutional arrangements in the EU appear to either accord exclusive rights to, or effectively favor, EU entities in the development and implementation of such measures. Further, there appears to be no effective mechanisms to ensure accountability to non-EU interests in the adoption and implementation of such measures;

- U.S. producers and exporters – particularly those without an established presence in the EU – are often disadvantaged by the technical and administrative requirements that result from the EU's promulgation of standards, conformity assessment procedures and regulations in inflexible, closed systems. U.S. exports can be further limited by third country adoption of EU standards and regulations as a result of their bilateral trade agreements with the EU and EU technical assistance; and

- Efforts to enhance regulatory compatibility and standards alignment between the United States and the EU have often been frustrated by a lack of clarity and transparency regarding EU decision making processes; lack of consistency and accountability regarding adherence to science and evidence based decision making; and lack of flexibility to consider standards of global relevance if they have been promulgated in a setting outside Europe. For example, the EU limits the array of standards that it recognizes, often leading to the EU adopting and implementing standards-related measures that lack market relevance, and are not sufficiently performance oriented or evidence based.

Accordingly, the overarching U.S. objectives in negotiations on regulatory issues in T-TIP are to achieve commitments that will lead to greater openness in regulatory and standards-development, risk analysis, impact assessment, and conformity assessment processes. U.S. producers, exporters and citizens possess important information, perspectives and ideas that – if taken into account by EU regulatory authorities in a timely, effective and accountable manner – could help ensure mutually beneficial outcomes. In the U.S. view, T-TIP presents an opportunity to move towards a more integrated transatlantic marketplace and a more compatible U.S.-EU approach to the development of standards and regulations in the United States and the EU and in third countries. T-TIP also presents an opportunity to explore how procedural openness and accountability throughout the regulatory rulemaking process can assist and support the achievement of greater alignment in specific sectors.

Indeed, in public remarks on September 30, 2013, U.S. Trade Representative Froman stressed that T-TIP must address differences in the U.S. and EU approaches to standards and regulations that have created unnecessary barriers – raising costs, deterring trade and investment, and negatively affecting our competitiveness and our consumers. He stressed that standards and regulatory issues have emerged as the greatest potential impediment to further integration of the world's two largest markets, and stated that T-TIP should embed the principles of transparency, participation and accountability to produce better regulations and mitigate many of the tensions the United States and EU face around regulatory divergences. Specifically, he noted the importance of:

- Transparency: Providing adequate advance notice of specific regulatory measures, not just preliminary, general papers on the subject, but the actual rule being proposed;

- Participation: Providing meaningful opportunities for input from a broad range of stakeholders, public and private, foreign and domestic; and

- Accountability: Providing responses to that input, a rationale for the final regulatory decision, based on evidence and science, including an impact analysis of the proposed regulation.

In 2013, the United States pursued these objectives through three rounds of negotiations. In 2014, we will continue to pursue the objective of reducing unnecessary regulatory barriers to trade while maintaining our high levels of health, safety, and environmental protection, and expanding transatlantic opportunities for U.S. producers and exporters. In addition, the public will continue to have an important role in continuing to shape our negotiating objectives. While the regulatory issues in T-TIP present considerable challenges, the United States is committed to reaching an ambitious, comprehensive agreement.

Free Trade Agreement – TBT Chapter Meeting

The inaugural meeting of the United States-Peru Trade Promotion Agreement's Committee on Technical Barriers to Trade was held in Washington, DC, on September 26, 2013. The two governments discussed their respective systems as well as particular issues such as nutritional labeling and use of biotechnology. The Peruvian delegation also visited dozens of stakeholders, and several regulatory agencies including the U.S. Food and Drug Administration (FDA) and CPSC, under USAID's Standards Alliance Program.

Regulatory Cooperation Fora

Executive Order 13609

On May 1, 2012, President Barack Obama signed Executive Order (E.O.) 13609 entitled *Promoting International Regulatory Cooperation* to help reduce, eliminate, and prevent unnecessary differences in regulatory requirements imposed by U.S. and foreign regulators, which can limit the ability of American businesses to export and compete internationally. The E.O. calls for the Regulatory Working Group established by E.O. 12866, and reaffirmed by E.O. 13563, to serve as a forum to discuss, coordinate, and develop a common understanding among agencies of U.S. Government positions and priorities with respect to: international regulatory cooperation activities that are reasonably anticipated to lead to significant regulatory actions; efforts across the Federal Government to support significant, cross cutting international regulatory cooperation activities; and promotion of good regulatory practices internationally, as well as the promotion of U.S. regulatory approaches, as appropriate.

USTR continues to lead on the coordination and development of standards-related trade policies. The United States participates in three bilateral regulatory cooperation forums aimed at promoting regulatory best practices and aligning regulatory approaches in economically significant sectors with the European Union, Canada, and Mexico.

European Union

The EU's approach to standards-related measures (as described in the 2012 TBT Report), and its efforts to encourage governments around the world to adopt its approach, presents a strategic challenge for the United States in the area of standards-related measures. In 2013, U.S. officials will continue to encourage systemic changes in the EU approach in existing bilateral fora, such as the Transatlantic Economic Council (TEC) and the United States – European Union High- Level Regulatory Cooperation Forum (HLRCF). The TEC is designed to give high-level political direction to bilateral initiatives aimed at promoting increased bilateral trade, job creation, and economic growth through deeper transatlantic economic integration. The HLRCF, comprising U.S. and EU regulatory and policy officials, oversees a program of bilateral cooperation on regulatory issues. The group has convened in advance of each of the previous four TEC meetings to identify projects for the TEC to consider.

Mexico

In May 2010, President Obama and Mexican President Calderón committed to enhance significantly the economic competitiveness and the economic wellbeing of the United States and Mexico through improved regulatory cooperation. The Presidents directed the creation of United States – Mexico High-Level Regulatory Cooperation Council (HLRCC), comprising senior-level regulatory, trade, and foreign affairs officials from each country.

In February 2012, the HLRCC released its first work plan, which outlines cooperative activities on food safety, electronic import and export certificates, oil and gas development, nanotechnology, motor vehicle safety, and e-health and conformity assessment. On October15, 2012, the HLRCC met to review progress on the seven work plans. It is expected a new consultation schedule will commence in 2013 to update the activities of the HLRCC.

The HLRCC reconvened August 15-16, 2013 in Mexico City to discuss progress of the seven work plans, and discuss the path forward for a new biennial work plan which will be drafted and finalized in 2014 for implementation in 2015.[43]

Canada

In February 2011, President Obama and Canadian Prime Minister Harper directed the creation of a United States – Canada Regulatory Cooperation Council (RCC), composed of senior regulatory, trade, and foreign affairs officials from each government. The RCC has a mandate to promote economic growth, job creation, and benefits to U.S. and Canadian consumers and businesses by enhancing regulatory transparency and coordination, with a focus on sectors characterized by high levels of integration, significant growth potential, and rapidly evolving technologies. The RCC website provides information on specifics for the 29 initiatives and work plans, including cooperation on topics such as, agriculture, personal care products, pharmaceuticals, and motor vehicles.

The RCC issued a Progress Report to Leaders on December 14, 2012. The report highlighted that work is also underway on the development of Memoranda of Understanding, discussion papers, initial statements of work on regulatory changes, and various assessment activities.

The RCC met in Washington, D.C., on June 19, 2013, to discuss work under the 2011 Joint Action Plan, the next steps in furthering United States-Canada regulatory alignment, and the role of the Council moving forward.

North American Leaders Summit – Trilateral Regulatory Cooperation

On February 19, 2014, President Obama met in Toluca, Mexico, with President Peña Nieto of Mexico and Prime Minister Stephen Harper of Canada for the North American Leaders Summit.

---

[43] The U.S.-Mexico HLRCC work plan can be found at

http://www.whitehouse.gov/sites/default/files/omb/oira/irc/united-states-mexico-high-level-regulatory-cooperation-council-work-plan.pdf

They discussed their vision for a prosperous and secure future for the citizens of all three countries and their shared commitment to work together to realize that vision. They announced concrete initiatives by the three countries aimed at enhancing North American competitiveness in the global economy, expanding opportunities for citizens, and promoting peace, security, and development through multilateral action. Some of these initiatives include: strengthening trilateral regulatory cooperation in order to ease burdens on business, including establishing in-country exchanges of regulators, and creating an outreach mechanism to increase stakeholder input, including from civil society.

X. COUNTRY REPORTS

Argentina

Bilateral Engagement

The United States raises TBT matters with Argentina during WTO TBT Committee meetings.

Testing Requirements for Lead in Graphic Products (Resolution 453)

As previously reported in the 2013 TBT report, the United States continues to be concerned with Argentina's Resolution 453/2010, which requires all inks, lacquers and varnishes used in producing printed materials, such as package labeling and inserts, to undergo testing for lead content. Resolution 453/2010 required testing to be conducted in one of two designated laboratories in Argentina. The United States expressed concern during WTO TBT Committee meetings in November 2011 and March 2012 that this resolution appeared to apply to foreign producers only, and that Argentina's testing capacity was insufficient to perform all the required testing. The United States asserted that the situation, coupled with the inability to test these products in the country of production, would lead to significant delays, cost and burdens for industry.

In March 2012, Argentina notified an amendment to Resolution 453/2010. Under this amendment, Argentina temporarily accepted a sworn declaration from the producer or importer stating that the product, or group of similar products, complies with the applicable norm, ASTM D 3335-85a, in lieu of testing at the designated laboratories in Argentina. In September 2012, Argentina also exempted from Resolution 453/2010 testing requirements for all printed materials destined for distribution or use in fairs, exhibitions, or other events that are declared "of interest" by the Ministry of Tourism. This alternative procedure, however, phased out in stages, and ended in November 2013.

Both the United States and the European Union raised concerns with this testing requirement during the March and June 2012 WTO TBT Committee meetings. The United States indicated that it continues to question whether mandatory third party testing should be required for these products since they are low risk, and whether it is necessary for the testing to be performed in Argentina itself or instead could be performed by any accredited laboratory. The United States will continue to press Argentina on this issue in 2014.

Electrical and Electronic Products – Conformity Assessment Procedures

Argentina's new requirements for conformity assessment for electrical and electronic products, modifying Resolution 92/98, became effective January 1, 2013, but Argentina has not notified the resolution modification to the WTO. The modified Resolution 92/98 specifies the process by which foreign manufacturers and importers obtain the S-mark safety certification from local certification bodies. This certification is required to market electrical and electronic products between 50 and

1000 Vac in Argentina.

According to U.S. industry, changes to Resolution 92/98 impose repetitive testing and associated delays, resulting in costs for U.S. exporters that outweigh the purported safety benefits. An importer with a recognized foreign certificate that had served as a basis for certification under Resolution 92/98 must now also have the product tested locally. This requirement is mandatory for all electrical products, rather than a class of electrical products based on risk. In addition, industry reports that the requirements disproportionately impact foreign manufacturers and importers and favor domestic manufacturers. Failure to follow Resolution 92/98 results in products not clearing customs and entering Argentina's market.

The United States will continue to press Argentina on this issue in 2014.

Brazil

Bilateral Engagement

The United States and Brazil discuss TBT-related matters in various bilateral fora, including the Commercial Dialogue led by Brazil's Ministry of Development, Industry, and Commerce (MDIC) and the U.S. Department of Commerce. Bilateral engagement also includes the Economic Partnership Dialogue between the Department of State and the Ministry of External Relations and the Commission on Economic and Trade Relations under the Agreement on Trade and Economic Cooperation (ATEC) between USTR and MDIC and the Ministry of External Affairs. The two governments also liaise during WTO TBT Committee meetings.

Medical Devices – GMP Certificates

As discussed in previous TBT Reports, the United States continues to be concerned with delays in registering medical devices in Brazil. Resolutions 24 and 25, notified to the WTO in May 2009 and also known as Public Consultation 11, establish the requirements for manufacturers to submit a Certificate of Good Manufacturing Practice for registration of health products. Resolutions 24 and 25 define a health product as a product that fits into one of two categories, either a medical product or a product for in vitro use diagnosis. As of May 2010, applicants have had to submit to Brazil's National Health Surveillance Agency (ANVISA), a Good Manufacturing Practices (GMP) certificate with their application for registration of health products in Brazil. ANVISA issues a GMP certificate only after it has inspected the manufacturing premises. A manufacturer must obtain the GMP certificate to access the Brazilian market, however, according to discussions in the 2013 WTO TBT Committee meetings, the average waiting time from submitting the inspection request until completing the inspection is twenty months, while U.S. industry reports a wait time of up to three years. This is significantly longer than the average time of three months for similar inspections performed by other accredited auditing bodies. This delay hinders medical device exports to Brazil.

The United States and other WTO Members raised this issue with Brazil at all three meetings of the WTO TBT Committee in 2013. The United States pressed ANVISA to accept existing GMP certificates without inspection or to consider subcontracting overseas inspections to accredited auditing bodies.

Brazil published Decree 8077 in the Brazilian Official Gazette on 14 August 2013, revoking Decree 79094 of 1977. With this new Decree, ANVISA gained autonomy to define products that would require GMP certification for registration, and those cases in which other health authorities or accredited bodies' inspection reports could issue the required GMP certification.

On November 12, 2013 Brazil notified Draft Resolution 50 to the WTO, which establishes requirements to prove compliance with GMP for registration of medical devices in Brazil. Brazil did not indicate an implementation date.

In January 2014 the U.S. FDA, the Australian Therapeutic Goods Administration, ANVISA, and the Canadian Health Products and Food Branch began a test of pilot single auditing project to strengthen existing mutual cooperation in the scientific and regulatory area of medical devices through the development of the Medical Device Single Audit Program (MDSAP). Specifically, MDSAP will allow recognized auditing organizations to conduct a single audit of a medical device manufacturer that will satisfy the relevant requirements of the medical device regulatory authorities participating in the pilot program.

While the MDSAP program is a promising step towards resolving concerns regarding Brazil's GMP certification requirements, industry reports that staffing shortages continue to delay the registration necessary to sell medical products in Brazil. In 2013, ANVISA hired and is now training more than 300 professionals to expedite the registration process. Brazil has also deputized state health inspectors to conduct international inspections.

In 2014 the United States will continue to monitor the implementation of medical device registration requirements in Brazil.

Telecommunications – Acceptance of Test Results

As discussed in the 2013 TBT Report, the United States continues to be concerned about Resolution 323 (November 2002) promulgated by Brazil's National Telecommunications Regulatory Agency. Resolution 323, Standard for Certification of Telecommunications Products, requires that in order to place products on the market in Brazil products be tested in Brazil, except in cases where the equipment is too large or too costly to transport. As a result, U.S. suppliers must present virtually all of their information technology and telecommunications equipment for testing at laboratories located in Brazil before that equipment can be placed on the Brazilian market. This requirement causes redundant testing, higher costs, and delayed time to market. Brazil did not notify Resolution 323 to the WTO.

The United States has urged Brazil to implement the Inter-American Telecommunication

Commission (CITEL) MRA with respect to the United States. Under the CITEL MRA, two or more CITEL participants may agree to provide for the mutual recognition of conformity assessment bodies and mutual acceptance of the results of testing and equipment certification procedures undertaken by those bodies in assessing the conformity of telecommunications equipment to the importing country's technical regulations. The United States and Brazil are both participants in CITEL. If Brazil implemented the CITEL MRA with respect to the United States, it would benefit U.S. suppliers seeking to sell telecommunications equipment into the Brazilian market by enabling them to have their products tested and certified in the United States to Brazil's technical requirements, eliminating the need for U.S. suppliers to have their products tested and certified in Brazil. The United States continued in 2013 to encourage Brazil to implement the CITEL MRA with respect to the United States, and will continue engagement with Brazil to this end in 2014.

Chile

Bilateral Engagement

The United States and Chile discuss TBT related matters in the context of the United States – Chile Free Trade Agreement, during annual Free Trade Commission and TBT Chapter Committee meetings, as well as during the WTO TBT Committee meetings.

Nutritional Labelling and Food Advertising

The Chilean Congress adopted Law No. 20,606 on nutrition and composition of food and food advertising on July 6, 2012, and the Chilean Ministry of Health (MOH) published the corresponding final implementing regulations in Chile's Official Journal on December 17, 2013. The regulations will be implemented in stages beginning June 17, 2014. The implementing regulations set limits for maximum levels of certain nutrients including saturated fat, calories, sugar, and sodium according to portion size of specific foods. Chile set nutrient limits for 24 categories of foods, including those preferred by children. If the limits in the food categories are exceeded, an icon must be placed on the front label panel, indicating the product is "High In" that nutrient. The icon must account for approximately 7.5 percent of the total surface of the packaging. Trade in processed and packaged foods to Chile amounts to $255 million annually. Chile notified the draft implementing regulations and accompanying guidance on advertising to the WTO.

The United States delivered initial WTO TBT comments on February 26, 2013 on a proposed version of the implementing regulations. The United States discussed this issue with Chile in the framework of the WTO TBT Committee, the United States – Chile FTA, on the margins of the TPP Agreement negotiations, and with senior level officials in Santiago. Other countries shared U.S. concerns over the proposed labeling requirements. Eleven countries, including the United States, expressed concerns at the June 2013 WTO TBT Committee, and eight countries, including the United States, spoke at the October 2013 TBT WTO Committee.

After this engagement, when Chile published the final implementing regulations in December 2013, they contained significant improvements over previous draft versions. Chile has decreased the total size of the icon from 20 percent of the total surface of the package to 7.5 percent. There is a choice of background colors of the square (red, blue, or green) where previously red or black was dictated. The font for the "High In" declaration is normal where previously it was bold and exaggerated. The Ministry of Health declaration inside the icon has been replaced with a statement that ties the icon to 2003 World Health Organization (WHO) diet recommendations.

Chile also reduced the number of food categories subject to the requirements substantially from its original proposal. According to industry, roughly 80 percent of all prepackaged foods might have needed the "High In" icons. In narrowing the scope of the food categories, however, Chile created questions about the scientific basis for food category selection. Chile also created concerns about how it will categorize domestic foods versus imported prepackaged foods. The MOH also made some improvements to the nutrient thresholds for yogurt and bread and standardized the majority of the nutrient thresholds at 20 percent of the daily recommended value for the nutrient.

The MOH authorities also responded positively to U.S. comments with respect to other aspects of the regulations, confirming that 1) foods served in restaurants will not be subject to the labeling requirements; 2) existing commercial inventories will not be subject to the labeling requirements, and 3) food importers can comply with the law by using supplemental labels or stickers.

The United States is pleased with modifications Chile made to the initial labeling proposal but remains concerned that Chile has adopted a staggered implementation approach, as opposed to giving 18 months for compliance for all foods. Some foods must comply in only six months, contributing to higher food production costs by limiting time for label redesign and use of existing labeling stock. Consumers may also interpret the six-sided icon on the package as a stop sign that will discourage consumption even when the product is consumed in the context of an overall healthy diet and active lifestyle. The United States will continue to monitor the situation, especially the trade impact on imported prepackaged foods, and seek opportunities to work with Chile both bilaterally and in the WTO TBT Committee to address remaining concerns.

Printers –Safety and Energy Efficiency Labeling

In August 2012, Chile notified to the WTO measures concerning "Safety for Printers" and "Energy Efficiency for Printers." These measures address safety and standby energy efficiency labeling for printers and require printers to be certified by a third party laboratory in Chile in order to be sold in Chile. Chile postponed the effective date to March 27, 2014, for the safety protocol and June 27, 2014, for the energy efficiency protocol. In December 2013, Chile also noted its intention to measure sleep versus standby mode for the energy efficiency protocol.

It is unclear what will happen to existing inventory already in the marketplace that do not meet these requirements. Also, U.S. industry will need additional time to come into compliance; U.S. industry believes that implementation needs to be delayed at least one year after Chile finalizes the measures. U.S. industry is also concerned that Chile did not take its comments into account. U.S.

industry submitted comments in October 2012, and did not receive a reply until April 2013, well after the comment period was over. The United States raised this issue both bilaterally and multilaterally on the floor of the WTO TBT Committee in 2013, and will continue to engage with Chile in 2014 to ensure that these requirements do not impose undue burdens on U.S. exports.

Electrical Labeling, Testing and Certification Requirements

In August 2013, Chile notified to the WTO a draft Decree 298-2005, titled "Adoption of the certification regulations for electrical products and fuel products." The draft measure sets stringent requirements for labeling, testing and certifying products covered by the decree. Only three laboratories have been approved to certify products. The requirement for testing and certifying printers appears duplicative given other measures Chile maintains that already require testing and certification of printers *(see previous entry)*. In addition, U.S. industry considers the labeling of each product with specific certification numbers and QR Codes as required under the decree to be especially burdensome. Chile stated that it would analyze comments through December 2013 and expects the decree to become effective in August 2014. In November, 2013, Chile put a hold on the process to revise Decree 298 in order to receive additional input and allow participation from stakeholders. The United States raised this issue both bilaterally and multilaterally on the floor of the WTO TBT Committee in 2013, and will continue to engage with Chile in 2014 to avoid unnecessarily burdensome labeling requirements.

China

Bilateral Engagement

In addition to discussing TBT issues in the WTO TBT Committee, the United States and China regularly engage on TBT related issues through the United States – China Joint Commission on Commerce and Trade (JCCT) and bilaterally on a case by case basis as specific market access issues arise. The JCCT, which was established in 1983, is the main forum for addressing bilateral trade matters and promoting commercial opportunities between the United States and China. The JCCT has played a key role in helping to resolve bilateral TBT issues, including those related to medical device recalls and registration, certification of information technology products, and cotton registration requirements.

China Compulsory Certification Requirements – Conformity Assessment Procedures

China's Certification and Accreditation Administration (CNCA) requires a single safety mark – the China Compulsory Certification (CCC) mark – to be used for both Chinese and foreign products. U.S. companies continue to report, however, that China is applying the CCC mark requirements inconsistently and that many Chinese produced goods continue to be sold without the mark. In addition, U.S. companies in some sectors continue to express concerns about duplication of safety certification requirements, particularly for radio and telecommunications equipment, medical equipment, and automobiles.

To date, China has authorized 152 Chinese labs to perform safety tests and accredited 13 Chinese certification bodies to certify products as qualifying for the CCC mark, as reported in the 2012 USTR Report to Congress on China. When it joined the WTO, China committed to provide nondiscriminatory treatment to majority foreign owned conformity assessment bodies seeking to operate in China. China rejected suggestions that it recognize laboratories that have been accredited by ILAC MRA signatories or develop other procedures to recognize foreign conformity assessment bodies. It insists that it will accept conformity assessment bodies domiciled abroad only if the governments of ILAC MRA signatories negotiate MRAs with China. Moreover, China has not developed any alternative, less trade restrictive approaches to third party certification, such as recognition of a supplier's self-certification.

Because China requires testing for a wide range of products, and all such testing for the CCC mark must be conducted in China, U.S. exporters are often required to submit their products to Chinese laboratories for tests that may be unwarranted or have already been performed abroad. This results in greater expense and a longer time to market. In addition, China has limitations on foreign invested conformity assessment bodies in country.

The United States has repeatedly raised its concerns about the CCC mark system and China's restrictions on foreign invested conformity assessment bodies with China both bilaterally and during WTO TBT Committee meetings. At the December 2012 JCCT meeting, China confirmed that eligible foreign invested testing and certification entities registered in China can participate in CCC mark related work and that China's review of applications from foreign invested entities will use the same criteria as those applicable to Chinese domestic entities. In 2013, the United States pressed China to take action to implement its 2012 announcement that foreign invested entities are permitted in this sector. At the December 2013 JCCT meeting, China committed that, beginning in spring 2014, it will use the same conditions that are applicable to domestic entities when reviewing applications from foreign invested entities registered in China to be designated as CCC mark testing and certification organizations.

The United States will continue to press China on treating foreign invested entities equally with domestic entities in 2014.

Mobile Devices – WAPI Encryption Standards

The United States continues to have serious concerns regarding China's 2009 unpublished requirement that its WAPI wireless local area networks (WLAN) standard be used in mobile handsets, despite the growing commercial success of computer products in China that comply with the internationally recognized WiFi standard developed by the Institute of Electrical and Electronics Engineers .

In 2013, Ministry of Industry and Information Technology (MIIT) remained unwilling to approve any Internet enabled mobile handsets or similar handheld wireless devices unless the devices were WAPI enabled. The United States continued to raise concerns with this requirement, both bilaterally and in WTO TBT Committee meetings. The United States will vigorously pursue a resolution of this issue in 2014.

Mobile Devices – Draft Regulatory Framework

MIIT issued the "Draft Mobile Smart Terminal Administrative Measure" on April 10, 2012. The draft measure proposed to establish a new regulatory framework for the mobile device market. The United States raised concerns about the draft measure with China in April and May 2012. The United States expressed concern that the measure would impose numerous new obligations, technical mandates, and testing requirements on information technology and telecommunications hardware, operating systems, applications, app stores, and other related services, and that the scope and mandatory nature of these requirements appeared unprecedented among the major global markets for mobile smart devices.

On June 1, 2012, MIIT published the draft measure on its website, soliciting public comment for 30 days. In addition, in November 2012, China notified the draft measure to the WTO TBT Committee and indicated that it would accept comments for a 60 day period. Both the United States and affected industry submitted written comments on the measure. The United States and U.S. industry are concerned that the top down government mandated requirements contained in the measure are overly burdensome and could create significant trade barriers. Furthermore, the United States and U.S. industry are concerned that including numerous voluntary standards and testing requirements relating to smart terminals in the measure could create additional trade barriers if these voluntary standards become mandatory through MIIT's testing and certification process. At the December 2012 JCCT meeting, China confirmed that it would take all stakeholder views into full consideration in regard to regulating information technology and telecommunications hardware, operating systems, applications, app stores, and other related services. In November 2013, MIIT finalized and implemented the measure, along with two associated voluntary standards that did not take stakeholder views into account. In 2014, the United States will closely monitor developments regarding this measure and any trade barriers associated with China's regulation of information technology and telecommunications hardware, operating systems, applications, app stores, and other related services.

4G Telecommunications - ZUC Encryption Algorithm Standard

At the end of 2011 and into 2012, China unveiled an encryption algorithm (known as the ZUC standard), which was developed by a quasi-governmental Chinese research institute for use in 4G Long Term Evolution (LTE). The European Telecommunication Standards Institute 3rd Generation Partnership Project had approved ZUC as one of three voluntary encryption standards in September 2011. According to U.S. industry reports, MIIT, in concert with the State Encryption Management Bureau , informally announced in early 2012 that only domestically developed encryption algorithms, such as ZUC, would be allowed for use in the network equipment (mobile base stations) and mobile devices comprising 4G TD-LTE networks in China. In addition, industry analysis of two draft ZUC related standards published by MIIT suggests that burdensome and invasive testing procedures threatening companies' sensitive intellectual property could be required.

The United States urged China not to mandate any particular encryption standard for 4G LTE telecommunications equipment used on commercial networks, in line with its bilateral commitments and the global practice of allowing commercial telecommunications service providers to work with equipment vendors to determine which security standards to incorporate into their networks. The United States stated that any mandate to use a domestic encryption standard such as ZUC would appear to contravene a commitment that China made to its trading partners in 2000 stating that China would permit the use of foreign encryption standards in IT and telecommunication hardware and software for commercial use and that it would only impose strict "Chinese-only" encryption requirements on specialized IT products whose "core function" is encryption. Additionally, a ZUC mandate would appear inconsistent with China's 2010 JCCT commitment on technology neutrality. In 2010, China had agreed to take an open and transparent approach that allowed commercial telecommunication operators to choose which telecommunications equipment and encryption technologies and standards to use for their networks and not to provide preferential treatment to domestically produced standards or technology used in 3G or successor networks, so that operators could choose freely among whatever existing or new technologies might emerge to provide upgraded or advanced services.

The United States pressed China on this issue throughout the run up to the December 2012 JCCT meeting. At that meeting, China agreed that it will not mandate any particular encryption standard for commercial 4G LTE telecommunications equipment. In 2013, the United States worked to ensure that MIIT's voluntary testing and approval process for the ZUC 4G telecommunications equipment standards fully protected applicants' intellectual property by not requiring source code or other sensitive business confidential information to be provided during the approval process. At the December 2013 JCCT meeting, China committed that it will not require applicants to divulge source code or other sensitive business information in order to comply with the ZUC provisions in the MIIT application process for 4G devices. In 2014, the United States will closely monitor developments in this area.

IT Products – Multi-Level Protection Scheme

Beginning in 2010 and continuing through 2013, both bilaterally and during WTO TBT Committee meetings, the United States has raised concerns with China about its framework regulations for information security in critical infrastructure, known as the Multi-Level Protection Scheme (MLPS), issued in June 2007 by the Ministry of Public Security and MIIT. The MLPS regulations put in place guidelines to categorize information systems according to the extent of damage a breach in the system could pose to social order, the public interest, and national security. The MLPS regulations also appear to require buyers to comply with certain information security and encryption requirements that are referenced in the MLPS regulations.

MLPS regulations bar Chinese information systems graded level three and above from incorporating foreign products (China grades an information system with respect to its handling of national security information, with the most sensitive systems designated as level five). Systems labeled as grade level three and above, for instance, must solely contain products developed by Chinese information security companies and their key components must bear Chinese intellectual property. Moreover, companies making systems labeled as grade level three and above must disclose product source codes, encryption keys, and other confidential business information. To date, government agencies, firms in China's financial sector, Chinese telecommunications companies, Chinese companies operating the domestic power grid, educational institutions, and hospitals in China have issued hundreds of request for proposals (RFPs) incorporating MLPS requirements. These RFPs cover a wide range of information security software and hardware. By incorporating level three requirements, many RFPs rule out the purchase of foreign products.

Currently, China applies the MLPS regulations only in the context of these RFPs. If China issues implementing rules for the MLPS regulations to apply the rules broadly to commercial sector networks and IT infrastructure, those rules could adversely affect sales by U.S. information security technology providers in China. The United States urged China to notify the WTO of any MLPS implementing rules regarding equipment related requirements. At the December 2012 JCCT meeting, China indicated that it would begin the process of revising the MLPS regulations. It also agreed to discuss concerns raised by the United States during the revision process. Throughout 2013, using the JCCT process, the United States pressed China to fully and quickly implement its JCCT commitment to revise the MLPS regulations. In mid-2013, China indicated that it is working on revising the regulations. However, to date, China has not yet issued them. The United States will continue to urge China to refrain from adopting any measures that mandate information security testing and certification for commercial products or that condition the receipt of government preferences on where intellectual property is owned or developed.

Medical Devices – Conformity Assessment Procedures

The United States has expressed concerns over the past years regarding China's medical device registration requirements. The Legislative Affairs Office of the State Council has considered amendments to Order 276 "Regulation on Supervision and Administration of Medical Devices" and it released significant revisions in 2007, 2010, and in 2012. China has not notified these amendments to the WTO.

The most recent 2012 revision (third draft) of Order 276 continues to mandate country of origin registration, a requirement that prevents foreign manufacturers of medical devices from registering their products in China without prior marketing approval in the country of origin or country of legal manufacture. According to U.S. industry, this requirement has blocked or inordinately delayed sales of safe, high quality medical devices to the Chinese market because some manufacturers did not apply for marketing approval for certain products in the countries in which they were produced or in their home countries for reasons unconnected with product quality or safety. For example, producers may design particular medical devices specifically for patients in a third country, such as China, or may choose to produce them in a third country for export only. In these situations, a manufacturer would have no business reason to seek to have a particular device approved in its home country or the country of export and would likely forego that process to avoid the associated burdens of time and money. China continues to defend this requirement despite concerted efforts to resolve this issue.

The most recent version (third draft) of Order 276 also continue to reflect: (1) problematic product type testing (or "sample testing") requirements; (2) a burdensome reregistration process; and (3) the requirement that clinical trials be repeated in China in order to register products there. U.S. industry continues to advocate for the transition from end product type testing to a quality management system approach, as outlined in ISO standard 13485. Furthermore, while the latest draft increases the validity of a registration from four to five years, China's reregistration process continues to require fees and submissions comparable to the initial registration process.

With respect to the issue of in country clinical trials, at the 2010 JCCT Subgroup meeting, China's State Food and Drug Administration (SFDA) committed that China would accept clinical evidence from outside China and that China would not automatically mandate in country clinical trials for Class II and Class III devices. However, the latest revision of Order 276 proposed a waiver of in country clinical trials for Class I (lowest risk) devices only and the availability of clinical trial waivers for Class II and Class III devices remains unclear. In bilateral discussions with China in 2012, the United States urged China to meet with stakeholders to discuss their concerns. In 2013, the United States raised the issue with China in the WTO TBT Committee, and it will continue to monitor the development of revisions to Order 276 in 2014.

Imaging and Diagnostic Medical Equipment – Classification

Another source of concern relates to China's classification of imaging and diagnostic medical equipment. China classifies most imaging and diagnostic medical equipment as Class III. This classification represents the highest risk and therefore it is the most stringent classification for medical devices. This classification is problematic because it deviates from international practices and burdens manufacturers with additional requirements, such as conducting expensive and potentially unnecessary domestic clinical trials.

During the 2011 JCCT meeting, the United States urged China to place certain imaging and diagnostic medical equipment into a lower risk category. China's SFDA committed to issue, by June 2012, a complete list of x-ray equipment to be placed in a lower risk category and agreed to endeavor to release a draft for an in vitro (e.g., test tube) diagnostic equipment catalog for public comment by June 2012. Subsequently, in August 2012, SFDA revised and lowered the classification for four subcategories of imaging and diagnostic medical equipment under the "Classification Catalogue of Medical Devices," including certain medical ultrasonic instruments and related equipment, medical x-ray equipment, medical x-ray ancillary equipment and components, and medical radiation protective equipment and devices. The United States raised the issue of reclassifying additional products with China in 2013 in the WTO TBT Committee, and it will continue to monitor developments in 2014.

Patents Used in Chinese National Standards

In the State Council's Outline for the National Medium to Long-Term Science and Technology Development Plan (2006-2020) and in the 11th Five Year Plan (2006-2010) for Standardization Development of the Standardization Administration of China (SAC), China prioritized the development of national standards.

In November 2009, SAC circulated for public comment proposed "Provisional Rules Regarding Administration of the Establishment and Revision of National Standards Involving Patents." The provisional rules indicated that in principle a mandatory national standard should not incorporate patented technologies. The draft provisional rules also indicated that, when the use of patented technologies was needed, a compulsory license could result if the relevant government entity was unable to reach agreement with the patent holder. The United States provided comments opposing this and other aspects of the draft provisional rules, which did not take effect. In December 2012, SAC circulated new draft interim measures, omitting certain troubling aspects of the earlier draft, such as the compulsory license provision, but raising other concerns, including in its definition of the responsibilities and potential liabilities of individuals and organizations that participate in the formulation of revision of national standards. In early 2013, the United States provided comments to SAC on these and other concerns. In December 2013, China issued its interim rules. The United States is reviewing the interim rules and will continue to engage with China on this issue in 2014.

Cosmetics –Approval Procedures and Labeling Requirements

SFDA initiated a series of changes to China's cosmetics regulation after obtaining jurisdiction over the industry in 2008. SFDA imposed additional requirements on "new ingredients" in April 2010, and issued guidance on the application and evaluation of new cosmetic ingredients in 2011. These actions stalled the approval of cosmetics containing new ingredients. In fact, SFDA has approved only a handful of new ingredients since 2010. The United States, along with EU and Japan, continue to raise concerns regarding the application requirements at WTO TBT Committee meetings.

In December 2012, China notified "Cosmetics Label Instructions Regulations" and "Guidance for the Cosmetics Label Instructions," which propose new labeling requirements that are in addition to the two existing labeling requirements that apply to cosmetic products. In January 2013, U.S. industry submitted comments through the U.S. TBT Inquiry Point, arguing that the proposed regulation overlaps and conflicts with existing Chinese regulations, and creates an undue burden for the industry.

The United States is also monitoring possible implications of SFDA's efforts to create an inventory of "existing ingredients" that have been approved for use in cosmetics products in China. In September 2012, SFDA released for comment the "SFDA Notification: List of Raw Materials Already in Use in Cosmetics (Third Batch)." It released the first and second lists of materials in April and July 2012, respectively.

In 2014, the United States will urge China to continue dialogue with all interested parties regarding these measures and to take into account the comments received. China should also consider alternative measures that are more commensurate with the risks involved, such as post market surveillance and reliance on internationally recognized good manufacturing practices (GMPs). These alternatives could meet China's legitimate regulatory objectives with fewer disruptive effects on international trade.

Colombia

Bilateral Engagement

The United States discussed TBT matters with Colombia during and on the margins of WTO TBT Committee meetings, and in the TBT Chapter Committee of the United States – Colombia Trade Promotion Agreement. The second meeting of the TBT Chapter Committee will be scheduled in spring 2014.

Commercial Vehicles – Diesel Emission Standards

As raised in prior TBT Reports, the United States remains concerned about the Ministry of the Environment and Sustainable Development's draft resolution amending Resolution No. 910 of 2008, which has now been renamed Resolution 1111. On December 14, 2012, Colombia notified this proposed measure to the WTO. Resolution No. 1111 is proposed to go into effect on January 1, 2015, fifteen months later than the initial implementation date. This resolution states that the current commercial vehicles emission standards in Colombia, EPA 98 (a U.S. standard) and EURO III (an EU standard), will no longer be valid for new commercial vehicles seeking registration for sale in Colombia. Furthermore, this resolution states that EPA 04 and EURO IV emission standards will only be accepted for long haul semitrailers until December 2014. The draft resolution provides that by January 2015, all commercial vehicles seeking registration for sale in Colombia must meet EURO IV emission standard requirements. Given the design of some U.S. manufactured diesel truck engines, U.S. industry has expressed concern that using this EU standard would effectively exclude many U.S. heavy duty trucks from the Colombian market. Further, according to EcoPetrol, the Colombian state-run oil company, the fuel necessary to comply with the new standard will not be available nationwide until 2017. Additionally, U.S. manufactured diesel truck engines that meet the U.S. EPA 04 standard, which is more stringent than the EURO IV standard, already face restricted access to the Colombian market, because Colombia does not maintain adequate supplies of the high quality fuel needed for these high technology engines.

In 2013, the United States, and other concerned WTO Members, including Japan, Mexico and Canada, raised these issues during the March and June 2013 WTO TBT Committee meetings.

The United States will continue to monitor this issue in 2014, as manufacturers begin to implement Resolution No. 1111.

Certificates of Free Sale

In April 2013, U.S. processed food manufacturers began to voice concerns with Colombia's duplicative certification regulations, which require the provision of a Certificate of Free Sale for each imported product both at the time of registration and on a shipment by shipment basis as imports are received. As the United States worked with Colombia's National Institute of Food and Drug Monitoring (INVIMA) to relax these requirements, INVIMA revised requirements in Circular (#400-1239-13), but did not notify the WTO of its revisions, to indicate that future Certificates of Free Sale must include additional language to which no U.S. Federal agency will attest.

After receiving an overwhelming number of complaints from global trading partners, in August 2013 INVIMA rescinded the requirement to include additional language in the Certificates of Free Sale in another Circular (#400-1846-13), which was also not notified to the WTO. Although through the rescinding of this requirement, Colombia prevented what could have resulted in effectively stopping the flow of U.S. processed food product trade, concern remains that U.S. exporters of processed food products continue to be required to provide Certificates of Free Sale at multiple stages of the export process. U.S. exporters complain that the costs associated with obtaining multiple certificates is problematic, and that they often are unable to obtain the requested Certificates of Free Sale in time for the shipments due to a lack of resources in the agencies tasked with providing these certificates. The United States plans to continue engagement with Colombia on this issue in 2014.

Ecuador

The United States discusses TBT matters with Ecuador during and on the margins of the WTO TBT Committee meetings and bilaterally.

Resolution 116 - Product Certificate

In 2013, Ecuador enacted technical regulations for numerous products, including food products, cosmetics, spices, toys, and building materials. It appears some of these technical regulations, although notified to the WTO, went into force without an adequate amount of time for interested parties to provide comments. Establishing compliance with the criteria specified in these various relevant technical regulations is a condition for importation or sale of these products in Ecuador.

Ecuador's Foreign Trade Committee issued Resolution 116 on December 4, 2013. This resolution applies to 300 products and sets out requirements to demonstrate compliance with the various technical regulations. Resolution 116 was not notified to the WTO before it went into force. Resolution 116 requires commercial entities to obtain a Certificate of Recognition to demonstrate that their products conform to the criteria in the various technical regulations. The certificate of recognition can only come from a body certified by the Ecuadorian Accreditation Organization – which to date have only been Ecuadorian bodies. Besides the burden from not being able to obtain a certificate from bodies in the exporter's home country, the authorized Ecuadorian bodies appear to lack sufficient capacity to fulfill the demand for the certificates. As a result, exports to Ecuador are declining sharply. It also appears goods already exported to Ecuador are having difficulty clearing customs.

Stakeholders have raised concerns that Resolution 116 and the various technical regulations may be intended to address Ecuador's trade balance rather than address legitimate health or safety concerns. Certain Ecuadorean government officials have been reported as stating that these measures are part of a policy of import substitution.

U.S. Federal agencies have been closely following these developments and have been engaging with their Ecuadorean counterparts. In addition, USTR has raised it serious concerns with Resolution 116 and the various technical regulations with senior Ecuadorian officials. The United States intends to continue to raises these concerns with Ecuador in 2014, both bilaterally and in the WTO TBT Committee.

Processed Foods – Nutritional Labeling Requirements

On November 29, 2013, an agency in Ecuador's Ministry of Health, the National Agency of Regulation, Control and Sanitary Surveillance, published Executive Decree No. 4522. The decree applies to various processed food products and requires the products to be sold with particular labeling as set out in an Ecuadorean technical regulation, RTE-INEN-022. In particular, prepackaged foods that contain sugar, salt, and fat must have mandatory front of pack labeling. Additionally, an icon, which takes up about 1/6th of the container or package, will be required, with a bar that will reflect low, medium, or high nutrient content by each 100 grams in the food for salt, sugar, and fat. Such symbols are commonly referred to as traffic light symbols. For foods that are smaller than 14.4 cm, that have high levels of fat, sugar or sodium, the icon is not required, but an advisory message is required, "For your health, reduce the consumption of this product." An advisory statement is also required for foods that contain less than 50 percent "natural" content in them. Ecuador defines a "natural food" as "a food as presented in nature that has not been transformed." The decree also states that there are no costs to implement the new labeling requirements. Producers of the affected products have one year to comply with the new requirements.

According to RTE-INEN-022, any nutritional labeling requires laboratory testing to confirm the nutrient content of processed products. Initial reports are that the new labeling will not trigger the need for exporters to reapply for a Sanitary Registration from the Ecuadorean government, a process than could be potentially costly and burdensome, as it requires additional laboratory testing to confirm the ingredients and labels of the food products.

The United States requested that Ecuador notify its proposed amendment to the WTO on March 26, 2013. No draft has yet been notified to the WTO. Ecuador has argued the decree is a Ministerial Amendment and therefore not subject to WTO notification. The United States considers this change to be an amendment to a technical regulation that should be notified to the WTO.

In 2014 the United States will continue to follow this issue closely. In particular, the United States will press to ensure Ecuador maintains a transparent process that allows for consideration of comments from stakeholders at an early and appropriate stage and to clarify that Sanitary Registration will not be required as part of any new labeling regime if manufacturers have made no other changes to the food product.

Mandatory Labeling of Foods Derived From Biotechnology

On October 15, 2013, Ecuador published an amendment to Technical Regulation RTE INEN 022 "Labeling of Processed, Packed, and Packaged Food Products" which indicates that beginning May 15, 2014, mandatory labeling of "contains transgenics" will be enforced. The U.S. industry is concerned that imposing mandatory requirements to label food and beverage products with the statement "contains transgenics" will negatively impact bilateral trade. For foods derived from genetically engineered organisms that have been found to be substantially equivalent to conventional counterparts, mandating "contains transgenics" labeling may create an erroneous impression that the product is less safe than conventional products.

The United States has engaged bilaterally with Ecuador on this issue including at the sidelines of the WTO TBT Committee meeting in October 2013 and will continue to raise this issue in 2014. On February 20, 2014 the United States submitted comments requesting a clear definition of "contains transgenics." The United States requested clarification of the manner by which "testing for access to compliance," and "demonstration of compliance" will be carried out with regards to mandatory transgenics labeling. The United States will in particular monitor the development of implementing regulations that are being drafted by Ecuador's government agencies.

European Union

Bilateral Engagement

The United States and the EU engage on TBT-related matters in various fora, including the TBT Committee, the Transatlantic Economic Council (TEC) and the United States – European Union High-Level Regulatory Cooperation Forum (HLRCF). This engagement aims to minimize unnecessary barriers to U.S.-EU trade. It also aims to promote the importance of maintaining open and transparent regulatory and standards development processes in emerging markets, as well as jointly advocating on specific market access issues on behalf of U.S. and EU exporters.

The launch of negotiations for a T-TIP Agreement – a comprehensive trade and investment agreement – is providing new opportunities to address TBT-related issues with the EU. In addition to developing disciplines that build upon WTO TBT obligations to further prevent and eliminate unnecessary obstacles to trade, the negotiations provide the United States and the EU a regular opportunity to meet to seek to resolve specific trade concerns. See Section IX for details on T-TIP.

Semiconductors and Refrigeration Appliances — Regulation on Fluorinated

Greenhouse Gases (F-Gas)

The EU notified its proposed changes to its regulation (No. 842/2006) on fluorinated greenhouse gases (F-Gas) on February 7, 2013 as G/TBT/N/EU/91. The European Commission had already transmitted its proposal to the European Parliament and European Council before notifying WTO Members. Consistent with President Obama's Climate Action Plan regarding U.S. leadership on global efforts to phase down the consumption and production of climate damaging HFCs, the United States strongly supports the objectives of the EU's proposed regulation, including its proposed approach that combines both a phase down of hydrofluorocarbons (HFCs) and specific appliance bans. However, a particular ban contained in the proposed measure raised concerns for some U.S. household refrigerator manufacturers. Indeed, several U.S., Korean, and Japanese industry commenters on the proposed regulation raised concerns with particular product bans, tight timelines for implementation and the unwillingness of the EU to meet with some impacted industries.

The specific concern among household refrigerator appliance manufacturers was the EU's proposed change to its F-gas regulations to ban the use of HFCs with global warming potential (GWP) of 150 or more in residential refrigerators and freezers on January 1, 2015. While the U.S. appliance industry does not oppose the reduction of HFC use – indeed many companies have already adopted alternative substances – it does oppose particular product specific regulations and the aggressive 2015 timeline for implementation with respect to household refrigerators and freezers. Specifically, the U.S. appliance industry commenters cited significant and expensive changes to manufacturing processes necessary to produce goods compatible with hydrocarbon refrigerants for a few companies, including some U.S. SMEs, that had not yet adopted the alternative substances taken up by others (*e.g.,* more than 50 percent of current new production globally uses hydrocarbons (HC-600a)).

The EU's own impact assessment recommended against a ban on HFCs in domestic (residential) refrigeration because of its low effectiveness towards reducing GHG emissions, stating that "a strict regulatory instrument such as a ban would need to be justified with a substantial contribution to the EU's emission reduction targets." However, the EU decided to include this ban. Additionally, the U.S. appliance industry was extremely concerned with the lack of its ability to participate in the development of this proposal beyond a single public meeting. Specifically, the appliance industry stated that DG Climate Action rebuffed several of its attempts to discuss the EU's proposal. Further, as noted above, the Commission had already transmitted its proposed regulation to the European Parliament and European Council, before notifying WTO Members, and therefore the Commission would not take Members' comment into account by revising its proposed regulation.

U.S. semiconductor manufacturers stated that they have eliminated noncritical usage of HFC, but no alternative input can be used for certain production processes. In their view, the proposed HFC phasedown to 20 percent of their baseline will negatively affect semiconductor production in the industry in significant ways. Because of the semiconductor industry's technical requirements related to use of fluorine in manufacturing (the fluorine atom's stability is critical to get precise manufacturing, and has specific chemical properties and functionalities that are critical to five to six phases of the semiconductor production process), it sought an exemption for this specific use, so that it could maintain production. Further, the semiconductor industry is an insignificant player in terms of absolute emissions of F-gas, emitting less than 0.05 percent of total EU HFC emissions in recent years. Additionally, it is difficult to predict what types of HFCs will be required by the semiconductor industry, since technology quickly changes year to year and the type of F-gas needed depends on the product being manufactured. The total share of semiconductor production capacity located in Europe that is owned by U.S. headquartered firms is approximately 41 percent.

The United States raised these concerns at the WTO TBT Committee in June and October 2013, as well as bilaterally with the EU in December 2013. In January 2014, the European Parliament and Council reported the final text of the F-Gas regulation and repealed Regulation (EC) No 842/2006. The final regulation exempted semiconductor production, addressing the concerns that United States and the industry had raised with respect to semiconductors, but maintained the January 1, 2015 deadline on HFCs in residential refrigerators and freezers that will result in a ban on products from U.S. companies unless or until they transition their production lines over to an alternative refrigerants with a GWP 150 or less. Formal adoption of the legislation by the European Parliament is expected in the coming month.

Proposal for Categorization of Compounds as Endocrine Disruptors

Endocrine disruptors (EDs) are naturally occurring compounds or man-made substances that may mimic or interfere with the function of hormones in the body. When available in the environment, potential endocrine disruptors may turn on, shut off, or modify hormone activity, leading to adverse impacts on the normal functions of tissues and organs. Under existing EU legislation on chemicals, pesticides, and other products, the Commission was to develop measures related to EDs by the end of 2013. DG Environment is charged with developing the approach for regulating EDs and opted to follow an approach based on categorization; under which hazard based "cut-off criteria" would be established to determine products that could be removed from the market. The 2013 deadline was not met, and the EU now plans to conduct an impact assessment to evaluate a range of options for ED related measures, including the use of hazard based cutoff criteria, for inclusion in amendments to EU Registration, Evaluation, Authorization and Restriction of Chemicals (REACH), the EU Biocides Directive and the Plant Protection legislation.

In early November 2012, DG Environment released an initial proposal for the definition, identification, and categorization of EDs. Although this approach was intended to be applied first to EU Plant Protection Product regulations, the DG Environment proposal, if implemented, would later be applied to other EU regulatory programs, including REACH. The initial set of categories developed in November 2012 by DG Environment included four categories – Known EDs, Presumed EDs, Suspected EDs and Potential EDs – which it narrowed down to two categories in February 2013 – Known EDs and Suspected EDs. DG Environment circulated a document containing its initial set of categories to a variety of stakeholders including NGO's, industry, and the U.S Environmental Protection Agency (U.S. EPA) for comment.

U.S. industry, particularly the chemical and crop protection sectors, submitted comments opposing the hazard based categorization or cutoff criteria approach, which excludes relevant and internationally accepted scientific and toxicological criteria including (1) potency, (2) exposure, (3) lead toxicity, (4) severity, and (5) irreversibility. In addition, U.S. industry requested DG Environment to consider language in EU Regulation 1107/2009 that would not require a category based approach, and to reflect in its proposal "scientific criteria for the determination of endocrine disrupting properties." U.S. EPA participated in DG Environment's informal public consultations by providing technical comments on the November proposal.

U.S. EPA comments detailed the science based approach of its Endocrine Disruptor Screening Program (EDSP) for characterizing chemical availability, activity, and adversity relevant to possible endocrine disruptors. The U.S EPA's EDSP is screening and testing substances for availability and activity, before determining if further evidence is needed to determine if the weight of evidence indicates endocrine mediated adversity. The U.S. EPA bases its registration requirements on decisions on registration or reregistration with a risk based approach taking into account availability and exposure, as well as activity and hazard. Under DG Environment's proposal, a substance could be deregistered if it is assigned to a category that meets the (activity) cutoff, without considering real world risk and evaluating the weight of evidence indicating adversity. Chemical and crop protection industries are very concerned that a large number of substances will be affected by the new categories and withdrawn from the EU market as a result.

Industry is concerned because categorization and development of lists of chemicals according to categories such as "suspected EDs" based purely on availability and activity would likely precipitate decisions to stop using those products or promote the switch to alternatives whose health effects may be less well understood, without any scientific demonstration that the products cause harm. In addition, the decisions could have the effect of denying access to useful products and technologies and expose the public to unknown or potentially more serious risks. Further, the proposal provides no specific criteria to evaluate data sets to determine what the specific properties are, what responses would qualify, what methods should be used to assure scientific validity, or what magnitude of effects would be needed to meet these terms.

DG Environment had intended to finalize its hazard criteria for all EDs by the end of 2013. DG Health and Consumers is responsible for plant protection materials and was to develop criteria for those products. It requested an evaluation of the hazards of EDs from the European Food Safety Authority (EFSA), which published its "Scientific Opinion on the hazard assessment of endocrine disruptors" with specific attention given to food safety in March 2013. EFSA concluded that "EDs can therefore be treated like most other substances of concern for human health and the environment, *i.e.,* are subject to risk assessment and not only to hazard assessment." DG Environment cited inconsistencies in the EFSA report, but nonetheless believes that the EU's approach to ED hazard identification is consistent with EFSA recommendations.

In mid-2013, the Commission's Secretary General's office determined that the regulatory changes planned by DG Environment necessitated an impact assessment, including an opportunity for public consultation. Impact assessments that have been conducted by independent organizations suggest significant trade impacts from an approach based only on hazard criteria. The need for an impact assessment was reinforced by an open letter written to the Chief Scientific Officer to the President of the European Commission, by 71 renowned European toxicologists. The letter urged the Commission to reconsider its regulatory approach to EDs which would be taken "without adequate scientific evidence," and "would reverse current scientific and regulatory practices." The Commission is expected to publish a roadmap in early spring 2014 which will provide a framework for conducting the impact assessment. While it is not clear whether or not the roadmap will be notified through the WTO, the Commission has indicated that it will provide a notice and comment period of 60 days on the roadmap.

In 2013, the United States raised concerns with DG Environment's proposal on the categorization of endocrine disruptors bilaterally, as well as in the WTO TBT and SPS Committees in June and October, and welcomed the decision to conduct an impact assessment on the plant and biological issue. The United States has emphasized the need for active public participation and transparency, including the opportunity for public comment on draft impact assessments, proposed regulatory actions and the supporting scientific opinions, and to have those comments taken into account in finalizing any measure. In 2014, the United States will closely monitor developments on this issue.

Chemicals – Registration, Evaluation, Authorization and Restriction of Chemicals

The European Union regulation for the Registration, Evaluation and Authorization of Chemicals (REACH) began as a Communication from the Commission in 2001, "White Paper on Strategy for a future Chemicals Policy (REACH)." The European Parliament (Parliament) approved REACH and the Council of Ministers (Council) formally adopted it in December 2006. REACH entered into force on June 1, 2007, and will be fully implemented by 2015. REACH impacts virtually every industrial sector, from automobiles to textiles, because it regulates chemicals as a substance, in preparations, and in products. It imposes extensive registration, testing, and data requirements on tens of thousands of chemicals. REACH also subjects certain chemicals to an authorization process that would prohibit them from being placed on the EU market except as authorized for specific uses by the European Commission.

Concerns regarding REACH have been raised at every WTO TBT Committee meeting since 2003 by the United States and many other delegations including Argentina, Australia, Botswana, Brazil, Canada, Chile, China, Chinese Taipei Colombia, Costa Rica, Cuba, Dominican Republic, Ecuador, Egypt, El Salvador, India, Indonesia, Israel, Japan, the Republic of Korea, Kuwait, Malaysia, Mexico, Pakistan, Philippines, Qatar, Russian Federation, Saudi Arabia, Singapore, South Africa, Switzerland, Thailand, and Uruguay. Members have intervened with concerns that aspects of REACH are discriminatory, lack a legitimate rationale, and pose unnecessary obstacles to trade. Members have indicated the need for greater transparency in the development and implementation of REACH requirements, and frequently cite the need for further information and clarification, as well as problems producers have in understanding and complying with REACH's extensive registration and safety data information requirements. The United States has also raised its concerns regarding REACH directly with the EU and has worked with the European Chemicals Agency (ECHA) on specific technical issues.

In recent years, the United States has registered concerns in the WTO TBT Committee and bilaterally regarding *inter alia* the following requirements under REACH.

- Rules for manufacturers outside the EU to appoint "Only Representatives" (ORs): An OR is a natural or legal person established in the EU authorized to carry out the obligations that REACH imposes on importers. REACH bars U.S. producers from registering substances for use in the EU and thus must engage an OR for this purpose. The requirement for foreign producers to appoint an OR imposes substantial cost burdens on them that European manufacturers do not bear. It can be highly expensive to contract with an OR, thus placing an additional financial burden on the exportation of the chemicals to the EU.

- Data compensation issues in connection with the operation of Substance Information Exchange Forums (SIEFs): For each registered substance, REACH requires the formation of a SIEF. U.S. industry has raised concerns that the "lead registrant" for each SIEF may take commercial advantage of its position in dealing with other SIEF members, particularly SMEs. Under REACH rules, other SIEF members must negotiate with the lead registrant to register their chemicals. A lead registrant could take advantage of this situation by charging those members exorbitant registration fees, thereby driving some companies (especially SMEs) out of the EU market. The United States urged the EU to consider issuing guidance for cost-sharing that would place limits on what lead registrants can charge other SIEF members, thus preventing undue financial burdens on those members, especially SMEs.

- The varying interpretation of "article" across the EU Member states and European Chemicals Agency (ECHA): Under EU REACH, if a certain chemical (a substance of high concern, or SVHC) is present in an article at 0.1 percent or more in concentration in that article, then a manufacturer/importer must notify the ECHA. Different Member states have issued interpretations for how an "article" is defined at variance with ECHA's definition. The Member state definition then determines the chemicals which need to be notified in that Member state – resulting in differences across Member states with which companies must track and comply. The Commission, and the majority of the Member states, views every article, including assembled ones, as a single article. U.S. industry supports that position. However, a number of Member states, including Germany, Austria, Belgium, France, Sweden, Denmark, and Norway, have rejected the ECHA's interpretation through their national rulemaking process.

- The treatment of monomers and polymers under REACH: REACH requires polymer manufacturers and importers to register reacted monomers in many circumstances. This is problematic because reacted monomers no longer exist as individual substances in polymers and would not create exposure concerns in the EU. In addition, EU polymer manufacturers generally can rely on the registrations of their monomer suppliers and do not need to be individually registered. As a result, the reacted monomer registration requirement provides an incentive for distributors to stop importing polymers and switch to EU polymer suppliers. The United States has pressed the EU to eliminate the requirement to register reacted monomers in polymers entering the EU market.

The proliferation of nanomaterials registries across the EU Member states: Among the substances subject to REACH regulations are nanomaterials, or "chemical substances or materials that are manufactured and used at a very small scale (down to 10,000 times smaller than the diameter of a human hair)," which are used in products ranging from batteries to antibacterial clothing. The Commission is considering options to adapt the data requirements for nanomaterials in REACH registration dossiers. An impact assessment is expected to be completed in spring 2014, and the Commission plans to propose amendments to the Council and Parliament by May or June 2014. The Commission plans to notify WTO Members per normal procedures, *i.e.*, after it puts forward its proposal for Co-Decision by the Council and Parliament.

Although REACH provides a standardized plan for reporting and registering nanoscale ingredients, several EU Member states have initiated the development of their own such registries, which often include exemptions for pigments and food additives. The Commission is preparing an impact assessment on transparency measures for nanomaterials, which will look at policy options to gather information on nanomaterials currently in the market, such as notification scheme or a registry. This would not necessarily be part of the REACH regulation. Plans are for the impact assessment to go to the Commission's Impact Assessment Board for review in the fall 2014. Given the EU Member states' access to REACH information on nanoscale ingredients, it is unclear how numerous national reporting schemes will help to deliver better knowledge or promote a more adequate and rapid response in the event of a specific risk being identified. Belgium, Denmark, France, and Italy either have instituted, or have announced plans to develop, a national registry. Industry questions the value that Member state level registries can bring, and expresses the following concerns: (1) the notification requirements in several Member states mandates submission of trade secrets or confidential business information; (2) variations in how Member states define a "nanomaterial" and its reporting requirements; (3) necessary time investment to understand and comply with the measures; (4) taxpayer expenditure in registry implementation; and (5) new administrative burdens.

- A lack of transparency and science based analysis associated with the *Community Rolling Action Plan* (CoRAP): The CoRAP is part of the REACH substance "evaluation" process. Its purpose is to allow EU Member states and ECHA to prioritize substances that are suspected of being hazardous to human health or the environment. Depending on the outcome of the evaluation, a substance evaluated under CoRAP may be considered for classification as a SVHC and become subject to authorization and restriction procedures. It is also possible that after evaluation, a substance will be found to not pose such a risk. ECHA has established criteria for selecting substances for placement on the list. These criteria address concerns about hazard, exposure, and tonnage. Member states are encouraged, but not obliged, to use the ECHA criteria and are empowered to evaluate the substances on the CoRAP list. The most recent CoRAP list was approved by ECHA on March 20, 2013. It operates over a three year period and is updated every March. The current list contains 115 substances, which will be evaluated during the course of 2013, 2014, and 2015. CORAP preliminary reports should be made available to interested U.S. companies, even if they have not yet registered the particular substance. Currently, the reports are only made available to registrants. More transparency on the part of the EU with respect to U.S. companies impacted by this regulation would reduce costs and address U.S. industry's concerns regarding the responsiveness of some Member states to their domestic interests in the CoRAP process.

In 2013, the United States also raised concerns bilaterally with the EU on the lack of public notice and comment associated with the "Risk Management Options" (RMO) analysis phase of the SVHC Roadmap. Under the Commission's Roadmap for evaluation of individual SVHCs, at the request of the Commission, a Member state Competent Authority or ECHA will conduct an RMO analysis to determine whether regulatory risk management is required for a given substance, and to identify the most appropriate regulatory instrument to address a concern. The regulatory decision may be to pursue authorization or restriction, address the concern via other legislation, or take no action. The Commission's SVHC Roadmap identifies five minimum criteria for the RMO analysis and states that the RMO is not meant to be public. Beyond this, the authority drafting the RMO has discretion with respect to the level of detail provided in its analysis and whether or not consultation of stakeholders is appropriate. ECHA has said that documenting the RMO analysis and sharing it with other EU Member states and the Commission promotes early discussion and should ultimately lead to a common understanding on the regulatory action pursued. The United States supports the EU's efforts to conduct RMO analysis, and believes the RMO analysis should be implemented in a harmonized and consistent manner by Member states. Further, regulatory decisions taken under this process carry the potential to significantly impact trade. To prevent or minimize potential adverse effects on trade, the RMO analysis should be subject to public notice and comment, with the views expressed by commenters taken into account by the Member state or ECHA irrespective of the domicile of the commenter.

Renewable Fuels -- Renewable Energy Directive

In April 2009, the EU adopted the RED (2009/28/EC), with the objective of helping lower its greenhouse gas emissions (GHG), reducing its dependence on foreign oil, and increasing rural development. The EU RED establishes mandatory national targets for the share of energy from renewable sources by 2020. It also establishes a methodology and accounting system by which EU Member states may record and calculate GHG savings as compared to a baseline for fossil fuels. According to the EU, this comparison quantifies the total amount of GHG savings in the EU and progress toward the EU's overall goal of a 20 percent reduction in GHG emissions versus 1990 levels by 2020. To count toward Member state specific renewable energy use targets, or benefit from incentives, the RED requires that biofuels and feedstocks for biofuels meet certain sustainability criteria. Combined with the Commission Communications 2010/C 160/01 and

2010/C 160/02 of June 2010, the RED also sets the reporting and verification requirements for obtaining sustainability certifications.

The United States and the EU agree that sustainable agricultural practices are a critical component in the expansion of food production needed in the future. However, we have expressed concerns both bilaterally and in the WTO that the RED, and its paperwork and verification requirements, is disrupting trade in U.S. products (specifically soybeans used as biofuel feedstock). Under Article 18(4) of the RED, which provides for bilateral agreements, the Commission and the United States jointly established the U.S.-EC Technical Working Group on the RED (TWG), to examine how long-standing U.S. conservation programs address RED sustainability criteria and create the framework for a bilateral agreement to accept U.S. exports of biofuel feedstock as compliant with the sustainability goals of the RED. During the final meetings of the TWG, the Commission stated that U.S. conservation laws and programs must be identical to those outlined in the RED sustainability criteria. At the TWG, the United States noted that requiring identical legislation raises questions under the WTO Agreement. The United States also contended that the results of U.S. conservation laws and programs address the RED sustainability criteria and provide verifiable compliance measures for mass balance accounting. The TWG agreed to suspend discussions on a specific RED bilateral agreement at the beginning of the T-TIP negotiations. In 2014, the United States will continue to raise concerns with the RED and press for a solution as T-TIP negotiations proceed.

The EU's RED continues to exert considerable uncertainty in global biofuel and biofuel feedstock markets, and to disrupt trade through a very narrow approach to assessing conformity with its sustainability criteria. The United States will continue to seek recognition from the EU of alternative approaches that can provide equivalent outcomes in ensuring sustainable production of biofuel feedstock. By recognizing the United States' longstanding environmental record, the EU could quickly realize our shared goals of cheaper, lower GHG emitting fuels and a significant increase in trans-Atlantic trade.

Transport Fuel -- Fuel Quality Directive

The EU's revised Fuel Quality Directive (FQD), adopted in 2009 as part of the EU's Climate and Energy package, requires fossil fuel suppliers to reduce the lifecycle greenhouse gas intensity of transport fuel by six percent by 2020. The Directive granted the Commission the power to develop a methodology for calculating the GHG life-cycle emissions for transport fuels. The United States strongly supports the goal of the FQD of reducing GHG emissions. We have, however, raised concerns with the Commission regarding the lack of transparency and opportunity for public comment in the development of the Commission proposal for the methodology for calculating the GHG life-cycle emissions for transport fuels.

Over the past eighteen months, DG Climate has prepared an impact assessment on different options for this methodology and held two stakeholder sessions on the impact assessment process itself. However, the draft impact assessment paper was not made public and there was no opportunity to comment on it. There is no detailed public information regarding implementation options under consideration by the Commission, or what the timeline for a final Commission proposal to the Council and Parliament will be. The lack of transparency in this process drew criticism from the United States, U.S. and European industry, and EU parliamentarians. The United States has raised these transparency issues bilaterally with the EU, including at the WTO TBT Committee.

Trucks – Maximum Authorized Dimensions

U.S. industry has long raised concerns that the EU's truck length requirements were too prescriptive and unnecessarily restrict U.S. exports of aerodynamic and fuel efficient trucks to Europe. On April 15, 2013, the EU issued a "Proposal for a Directive of the European Parliament and of the Council amending Directive 96/53/EC laying down for certain road vehicles circulating within the Community the maximum authorized dimensions in national and international traffic and the maximum authorized weights in international traffic." The EU notified the proposal to the WTO in G/TBT/N/EU/109 on May 24, 2013. The proposal stated that "in light of evolving market and available technologies" it is necessary to amend existing regulations (Directive 96/53/EC) "to improve the aerodynamics of vehicles and their energy efficiency, while continuing to improve road safety."

EU vehicle safety regulations measure truck lengths from the front bumper of the tractor to the rear of the trailer. The regulatory approach taken by the U.S. Department of Transportation is based on the length of the trailer. This regulatory divergence has driven the development of two, contrasting schools of truck design: streamlined aero-nosed products in the United States and shorter, blocky "cabovers" in the EU. In the EU, and among countries that have adopted EU's approach, the allowable length of a truck tractor-semitrailer combination is 16.5 meters. Because American aero-nosed truck tractors are approximately 1.5 meters longer than European cabover truck tractors, they must pull shorter semitrailers in order to meet the truck tractor-semitrailer combination limit of 16.5, which diminishes payload capacity. Thus, while the EU approach does not ban American aero-nosed truck tractors, they are economically disadvantaged, because every measured inch/centimeter of the tractor up front means less space for paying cargo. Although aero-nosed trucks are longer, they have many advantages over cabover trucks. The best aero-nosed tractor is over 19 percent more aerodynamic and over nine percent more fuel efficient than the best cabover. As a result, aero-nosed products emit fewer greenhouse gases.

The EU's proposal contained several elements to promote greater energy efficiency, including revisions that would allow truck tractor-semitrailer combinations to exceed 16.5 meters in length and to add flaps to the rear of the vehicle. The proposal also contained the statement: "The only purpose of these exceedances is to allow the addition to the rear of vehicles or vehicle combinations of devices increasing their aerodynamic characteristics." It was therefore unclear whether the EU's proposal would provide an opening to the longer American aero-nosed truck tractors regardless of whether devices were to be added at the rear. The Vice President of the European Commission has stated that the EU's "intention is precisely to allow the potential use of slightly larger, more aerodynamic tractors - and/or rear devices, at the choice of manufacturers and end-users" and this intention would be captured in the still-to-be-developed technical specifications on aerodynamic designs or rear devices for trucks.

Food – Labeling Requirements

EU framework regulation 1169/2011 on the provision of food information to consumers – published in the Official Journal on November 22, 2011 – combines several EU directives and establishes new horizontal food labeling requirements. Most provisions will apply from December 13, 2014, with mandatory nutrition labeling effective December 13, 2016. Although regulation 1169/2011 was adopted in December 2011, the EU still needs to propose and adopt a series of additional regulations to implement general provisions of the framework, and if necessary, conduct the corresponding impact assessments that normally accompany such proposals.

The United States has trade concerns regarding how certain elements of regulation 1169/2011 will be implemented, and is monitoring developments closely. The chief concern of U.S. industry is that regulation 1169/2011 appears to provide wide latitude for EU Member states to adopt non-uniform implementing regulations. U.S. industry is concerned about the burden of meeting multiple labeling requirements, particularly if those requirements cannot be met through stickering or supplemental labeling. During the consultative process, the United States sought assurances that imported products will be subject to harmonized EU requirements, regardless of port of entry, and that compliance with national schemes (such as the United Kingdom and Ireland's traffic light requirements) would remain voluntary.

The United States is working bilaterally to better understand the rationale and basis for mandatory labeling requirements that appear more stringent than those found in the Codex General Standard. The United States is also seeking assurances that only harmonized EU requirements will be mandatory and that national labeling requirements remain voluntary.

Agriculture Products – Quality Schemes

Traditionally, EU policies on agricultural quality have been developed on a piecemeal basis. On May 28, 2009, the European Commission published its "Communication on Agricultural Product Quality Policy" aimed at clarifying and simplifying its product quality policies. The Communication addresses EU quality schemes, marketing standards and other certification and labeling schemes, such as organics and animal welfare. It follows on from a Green Paper published in October 2008, and outlines a policy framework for three complimentary quality schemes: the geographical indication scheme, which consists of Protected Designation of Origin (PDO) and Protected Geographical Indication (PGI); the "Traditional Specialty Guaranteed" (TSG) scheme; and optional quality terms. Optional quality terms are defined as additional information about product qualities such as "first cold-pressed extra virgin olive oil" and "virgin olive oil." A separate measure addresses the marketing standards for wine and spirits, notified to the WTO on September 11, 2011.

The three quality schemes are either certification schemes for which detailed specifications have been laid down and which are checked periodically by a competent body; or labeling schemes which are subject to official controls and communicate the quality of a product to the consumer. Schemes can indicate that a product meets baseline requirements but can also be used to show "value-adding qualities" such as specific product characteristics or farming attributes (e.g. production method, place of farming, mountain product, environmental protection, animal welfare, organoleptic qualities, Fair Trade, etc.). Schemes can be voluntary or mandatory.

The United States submitted comments on the "Proposal for a Regulation of the European Parliament and of the Council on agricultural product quality schemes (COM (2010)733)" (notified as G/TBT/N/EEC/379) to the EU on August 2, 2011 and received a response from the EU in December of 2011. The United States asked the EU to clarify the level of specificity required to identify a "place of farming," as well as the legitimate objective for such a requirement. The U.S. comments also highlighted concerns that the proposal establishes a framework that provides a "legal basis" for expanding place of farming requirements to all processed products from specified commodities. The EU responded that "place of farming" will be applied on a case-by-case basis, following impact assessments, and further noted that the definition of "place of farming" will change from one product to another.

The European Parliament and Council finalized its regulation on quality schemes for agricultural products and foodstuffs EU 1151/2012 in November 2012. In order to implement its general provisions, 1151/2012 gives the Commission the power to adopt delegated or implementing acts, and the Commission has not yet issued such measures. The specific provisions in the expected delegated and implementing acts may create additional challenges for U.S. exporters.

The United States remains concerned that "place of farming" requirements are unclear and difficult to comply with, and lack a basis in international standards. Codex, for instance, maintains no recommendation for place of farming designations, and has rejected proposals that would have expanded country of origin designations to foods with multiple ingredients, because such labeling caused consumer confusion.

Further, the United States remains concerned over certain aspects of the TSG requirements, including whether "prior use of a name" includes a trademark or prior geographical indication. The United States is also seeking clarification of the manner of precedence in determining TSG requirements relative to trademarks. Despite assurances from the EU that the provisions of 1151/2012 "ensure that a prior trademark is not affected by the registration of a TSG," it remains unclear whether prior use of a trademark will be grounds for opposing registration of a TSG. Further, the EU has shortened the comment period to oppose a registration from six months to two months. The United States views two months as insufficient time to prepare a dossier to oppose a proposed PDO/PGI/TSG.

Wine – Traditional Terms

Separate from its policies on agricultural quality schemes, the EU continues to aggressively seek exclusive use of "traditional terms" such as "tawny, ruby, and chateau" on wine labels. Such exclusive use of traditional terms impedes U.S. wine exports to the EU. Wines with a trademark granted before 2005 can use the terms, but more recent products cannot. In December 2013, it will be more than three years since the U.S. industry submitted applications to be able to use the terms, with no final confirmation that the applications have been approved from the EU. The EU recently approved the U.S industry's applications for use of terms "cream" and "classic," but the EU's delayed application approval process for other terms raises questions about the consistency of this process with the TBT Agreement. The United States has raised this issue repeatedly in the WTO TBT Committee for several years, and beyond approving two terms, the EU has not taken any visible steps to address our concerns.

At the March 2013 EU-U.S. Wine Bilateral meeting, representatives from DG Agriculture and Rural Development (DG Agri) indicated that the EU would reform the application process. They acknowledged difficulties with the term-by-term approval process and that the Commission will undertake to apply a different approval procedure. The Commission did not provide any timeline for completing the application process reforms. In June 2013, the World Wine Trade Group (WWTG) expressed to DG Agri that WWTG countries, including the Argentina, Australia, Canada, Chile, Georgia, New Zealand, South Africa, and United States, are frustrated with the EU's application process, which seem to be more trade restrictive than necessary. The EU stated that it would take WWTG's considerations into account.

The United States continues to stress to the Commission that common usage names of products should not be absorbed into quality schemes, whether for wine or other products. If a Codex standard exists or if the name is used in a tariff schedule or by the World Customs Organization, the United States believes that the name should be excluded from the quality schemes. The United States has further pressed that new certification and labeling schemes not be required for market access; however, where the EU implements such schemes, efforts should be made to acknowledge voluntary U.S. industry definitions. Similarly, U.S. processes and procedures should be acceptable for labeling requirements and system and process comparability with industry definitions should be sought in order to minimize any negative market access impact for U.S. exports.

Distilled Spirits – Aging Requirements

The EU requires that for a product to be labeled "whiskey" it must be aged a minimum of three years. U.S. whiskey products that are aged for a shorter period cannot be marketed as "whiskey" in the EU market or other markets, such as Israel and Russia that adopt EU standards. The United States views a mandatory three-year aging requirement for whiskey as unwarranted. In fact, recent advances in barrel technology enable U.S. micro-distillers to reduce the aging time for whiskey. In 2014, the United States will continue to urge the EU and other trading partners to end whiskey aging requirements that serve as barriers to U.S. exports.

India

The United States discusses TBT matters with India during WTO TBT Committee meetings and on the margins of these meetings. The U.S. government also discusses such matters in bilateral meetings, including under the U.S.-India Trade Policy Forum and the U.S.-India Commercial Dialogue.

In addition, the U.S. Trade and Development Agency (USTDA) funds a program with the Confederation of Indian Industry (CII) to facilitate India's development of a transparent and more streamlined system of standards, conformity assessment, and technical regulations. ANSI's standards portal contains information regarding the U.S. and Indian standardization systems. (www.standardsportal.org).

Legal Metrology - Packaged Commodities Rules

The Legal Metrology (National Standards) Rules, 2011 issued by India's Department of Consumer Affairs have been in force since 2011. India first notified them to the WTO upon their third amendment on in 2012, which entered into force after just 40 days notification. The rules were further amended in June of 2013 and published in India's Gazette, however, India did not notify the amendment to the WTO, and the changes have now entered into force. These rules stipulate that all pre-packaged commodities are prohibited, unless they are in a standard quantity and carry all prescribed declarations. Varying interpretation and enforcement of the requirements, and conflicting provisions with labeling and packaging requirements maintained by Food Safety and Standards Authority (FSSAI) and the Ministry of Commerce (MOCI), have created an uncertain environment, causing detention of shipments at the port of entry and cancellation of import contracts. U.S. officials in New Delhi highlighted concerns to India's Secretary of Consumer Affairs in October 2013, and met with more than 21 other Ministries reporting similar detentions and trade challenges related to the Legal Metrology and FSSAI requirements.

Mandatory Container Sizes

The Legal Metrology Rules create mandatory package sizes in metric units excluding many U.S. food products from the market since they are packaged in traditional English units (fluid ounces, pounds, and pints). Highly impacted commodities include canned and bottled drinks, packaged biscuits and bottled vegetable oils. Mandatory package size requirements are not recommended by international standards. Net weight declaration, supported by Codex and other international bodies, better protects consumers from fraudulent packaging practices.

Wholesale Foods Labeling

The Legal Metrology standard also creates a definition for wholesale foods that is inconsistent with similar requirements laid out by FSSAI in the Food Safety and Standards Regulations (FSSR). Further, the measure requires that all products be labeled with dates of production, importation, and expiration and that at least 60 percent of a product's shelf life must remain at the time of importation. This has led Indian Customs officials to reject or detain shipments of unprocessed agricultural products, such as tree nuts and apples, which do not have a specific production date.

FSSR

The United States has detailed concerns about onerous India-specific labeling issues in previous TBT Reports since the FSSR were published in India's Gazette in 2011. India's responses have failed to provide additional or reliable information with regard to how the elements of this measure advances safety or efficacy or quality of the products in question or meets the specific needs of India. The United States continues to seek clarification about India's specific needs in those instances where the FSSR appears inconsistent with the Codex General Standard for the Labelling of Prepackaged Foods recommended practices or international practice.

In 2013, India established health advisory statements for glucose, plant stanol esters, and dietary fibers in the FSSR. The United States asked India in October 2013 to confirm if these advisory statements were needed for imported products and is awaiting a response. India also established in the FSSR requirements for the mandatory display of the FSSAI "license number" along with the FSSAI logo in the principal display panel of food package consignments. India did not notify the new requirements to the WTO. FSSAI confirmed in December 2013 that imports may comply with the license and logo labeling through the use of a sticker, however, the United States remains concerned that India continues to develop costly national level requirements.

The United States will continue to press India to resolve these issues in 2014.

Telecommunications Equipment – Security Regulations

In 2009 and 2010, India promulgated a number of regulations negatively impacting trade in telecommunications equipment, including policies on mandatory transfer of technology and source codes as well as burdensome testing and certification requirements for telecommunications equipment. While international stakeholders successfully lobbied India to roll back most of these measures, India retained the objective of testing all "security-sensitive" telecommunications equipment in India by April 2013. U.S. Government officials and U.S. industry have continued to press India to reconsider the domestic testing policy and to adopt the international best practice of using international common criteria and accepting products tested in any accredited laboratory in India or elsewhere. In October 2013, India announced that the domestic security testing deadline would be extended to July 1, 2014. However, there is no indication that India's domestic security testing capacity, which is currently very limited, will increase sufficiently by that time.

In February 2012, India announced a Preferential Market Access (PMA) policy for domestically manufactured telecommunications equipment. The policy stated that domestically manufactured equipment would receive preference in government procurement and in some types of private sector procurement owing to a combination of India's twin goals to expand its domestic manufacturing capacity and to protect the security of its telecommunications networks. Following significant engagement with the government of India by senior U.S. Government officials and U.S. industry,

India revised the PMA in December 2013. The revised policy continues to require that domestically manufactured goods constitute a certain percentage of the electronic products procured by government entities. The revised PMA policy also applies the same requirement to "procurement of electronic products made under all Centrally Sponsored Schemes and grants made by the Central Government."

The United States will continue to seek clarification on the scope and application of the revised PMA policy from the government of India and closely monitor its implementation in 2014.

Electronics and Information Technology Equipment – Safety Testing Requirements

U.S. electronics and IT goods manufacturers have raised concerns about the Indian Department of Electronics and Information Technology's (DEITY) September 2012 order that mandates compulsory registration for fifteen categories of imported electronic and IT goods. The policy, originally set to take effect April 2013, mandates exporters to register their products with laboratories affiliated or certified by the Bureau of Indian Standards (BIS). This is despite the fact that all U.S. electronic exports currently sold in India are fully certified in internationally recognized laboratories, and the government of India has never articulated how such a domestic certification requirement advances India's legitimate public safety objectives. Notwithstanding ongoing efforts by global industry to engage the government of India to resolve concerns and ambiguities in the policy without undermining those objectives, the Order entered into force in January 2014.

India currently has seven government and private laboratories accredited by BIS for testing and certification – far fewer than will be necessary to accommodate the high volume of electronic goods the country imports. Accordingly, enforcing these requirements could result in hundreds of millions of dollars' worth of U.S. exports being locked out of the Indian market, causing great concern for U.S. companies. To date, BIS has maintained that it will not recognize certification from laboratories located outside of India.

Although U.S. industry would ultimately like to see the entire policy repealed, an important first step is to seek an exemption for Highly Specialized Equipment (HSE), including servers, storage, printing machines, and IT products that are installed, operated, and maintained by professionals who are trained to manage the product's inherent safety risks. These products pose little risk to the general consumer public. U.S. companies have already incurred significant expenses due to testing samples being destroyed during the safety testing process in Indian labs. Indian test labs have also indicated that they do not have the capacity to test some products, that require industrial power supply, exceed household or office voltage, or are very large in size and weight. Moreover, exporters are forced to leave their products in these labs for extended and undefined periods of time.

USTR has been actively raising this issue bilaterally, in the WTO TBT Committee in 2013, and will continue to discuss with the Government of India in 2014.

Proposed Amendment to the Hazardous Waste Act

In 2008, India's Ministry of Environment and Forests (MoEF) adopted rules styled as the "Hazardous Wastes (Management, Handling and Transboundary Movement) Rules, 2008," which set forth requirements and procedures for the storage, handling, and disposal of hazardous waste. Following a number of amendments in the intervening years, in 2011 MoEF proposed further amendment to the Hazardous Wastes Rules, referred to by MoEF as the "Fifth Amendment." The proposed Fifth Amendment, published in November 2013, but not notified to the WTO, sets out conditions for the import and movement of used and refurbished electrical and electronic equipment (EEE). The United States fully supports the protection of the environment and health against adverse impacts of wastes. U.S. industry has expressed concerns that, under the proposed Fifth Amendment, hazardous waste controls on imports of used EEE for direct reuse and imports of refurbished EEE pursuant to a service warranty, and other similar controls on EEE, would impose unnecessary burdens on trade that facilitates reuse and extension of life of EEE to the benefit of the environment.

The United States will continue to press India to resolve these issues in 2014.

Indonesia

Bilateral Engagement

The United States discusses TBT matters with Indonesia both bilaterally and during WTO TBT Committee meetings and on the margins of such meetings. Additionally, the United States – Indonesia TIFA Council provides a forum for bilateral discussions on a variety of trade-related issues, including standards-related issues. The United States and Indonesia also participate actively on standards and conformity assessment issues through ASEAN and APEC. In June 2013, Indonesia and the United States co-hosted a workshop under USAID's Standards Alliance program aimed at promoting transparent, predictable, and effective regulatory practices that will encourage enhanced trade and investment.

Horticulture Products – Labeling Requirements

In September 2012, Indonesia issued Ministry of Agriculture's (MOA) Regulation 60 and Ministry of Trade's (MOT) Regulation 60 (amending MOT Regulation 30), which have since been replaced by MOA Regulation 86/2013 and MOT Regulation 16/2013, as amended by MOT Regulation 47/2013 in August 2013. These regulations impose a broad range of requirements on the importation of horticultural products into Indonesia and include provisions related to labeling and packaging that, among other elements, require that labels in the Bahasa language be attached to the packaging prior to entering the Indonesian customs area. Indonesia did not notify these regulations to the WTO TBT Committee. The United States had raised the issue of allowing supplemental labels to comply with Bahasa labeling requirements at the WTO TBT Committee during 2011 in regard to the September 1, 2010, Circular Letter HK.05.01.1.52.09.10.8502 from Indonesia

National Agency for Drug and Food Control. The United States will continue to raise concerns in 2014 regarding the labeling aspects of the measures.

Toys – Standards and Testing Requirements

In October 2013, Indonesia began enforcing a new mandatory toy standard – Ministry of Industry Regulation 24 of 2013 (SNI:8124:2010), despite expressions of concern and requests for delay made bilaterally and in the WTO TBT committee in 2013 by the United States and other trading partners. A particularly problematic aspect of the new regulation was a requirement that a manufacturer establish conformity through in-country testing in Indonesia. When hundreds of shipments of toys became stuck at Indonesian ports, Indonesia delayed enforcement of the regulation until April 2014. As part of the delay, Indonesia also announced that it would accept test reports from foreign ILAC-accredited laboratories for two years, after which the regulation will require a bilateral agreement to avoid in-country testing. Despite the delay, the U.S. toy industry remains concerned about technical requirements, such as the sampling and frequency of testing, as well as the future requirement for bilateral agreement to avoid in-country testing. The United States will remain engaged with Indonesia on this issue in 2014.

Cell Phones, Handhelds, Tablets and Laptops – Product Testing

Indonesia has issued a number of measures that make it more difficult to import cellular and WiFi-equipped products. In late 2012, Indonesia issued MOT Regulation 82, which was subsequently amended by MOT Regulation 38 in 2013, and Ministry of Industry (MOI) Regulation 108. Under these measures, to obtain an import license, companies must provide product identification numbers for each imported item, and receive: (1) an import certification from MOI; (2) a certification for telecommunication device and equipment from the Ministry of Communication and Information Technology (KOMINFO); and (3) a label in Bahasa.

In May 2013, KOMINFO published Postel Regulation 5, which imposes strict testing requirements on the devices, covered by MOT 82/2012, as well as notebooks and personal computers. This measure requires imported cell phones, tablets, handhelds, laptops, and other equipment with Bluetooth or wireless LAN features to be tested at the device-level rather than the more common modular-level. Further, tests must be conducted in Indonesian test labs. The Communications Ministry also requires companies to provide product identification numbers for each individual product to be imported. U.S. companies reported that they were unable to provide such numbers months in advance, as required by the measure. In response, the United States and other trading partners raised concerns with Indonesia regarding these new requirements, both bilaterally and in all three WTO TBT Committee meetings in 2013. The United States and U.S. companies also raised concerns with Indonesia on this issue. As a result, the Ministry delayed full implementation until January 2014.

The United States will remain engaged on these issues directly with Indonesia and by supporting more regularized consultations between U.S. industry and the Indonesian government.

Korea

Bilateral Engagement

Korea and the United States regularly discuss TBT issues during and on the margins of the WTO TBT Committee meetings, working groups set up under the United States – Korea Free Trade Agreement (KORUS) such as the Automotive Working Group, and through other bilateral consultations.

Chemicals – Act on the Registration and Evaluation of Chemicals

On May 22, 2013, the Act on the Registration and Evaluation of Chemicals became law. Under the law, manufacturers and importers of chemical substances subject to the law will be required to be registered and subject to annual reporting requirements. On February 18, 2014 Korea's Ministry of Environment released draft implementing regulations, which it plans to finalize by summer 2014, with expected entry into force on January 1 2015. The draft regulations allow simplified registration for new chemicals under 1 ton. Industry still has concerns about the high costs and potential release of sensitive business information involved with the Only Representative reporting system, and the regulation of chemicals registered in a "gap" period between 2012 and 2014. In 2014, the United States will continue to monitor developments and engage with Korean authorities to share concerns and to minimize or eliminate unwarranted burdens contained in the implementing regulations.

Organic Products – Requirements and Conformity Assessment Issues

Korea's Act on Promotion of Environment-Friendly Agriculture and Fisheries and Management and Support for Organic Products (the "Organic Act"), became effective on January 1, 2014. Under the Organic Act, U.S. processed organic exports to Korea are to be certified by a certifier accredited by Korea's Ministry of Agriculture, Food, and Rural Affairs as meeting particular standards in order to continue to be labeled as organic, and processed organic products will need to be recertified. Many U.S. producers and certifiers are reluctant to seek product re-certification under the Organic Act due to prohibitive costs and technical difficulties related to ingredient certifications and certifier readiness. However, the Organic Act permits the conclusion of equivalence agreements, which could potentially alleviate burdens on U.S. products and allow U.S. certified products to be labeled as organic in Korea without have to undergo re-certification by Korean authorities. Nevertheless, the Organic Act did not permit Korea to start the official negotiations on equivalence agreements before January 1, 2014 –creating a gap between the time U.S. organic exports will be subject to these requirements but before an agreement for equivalence can be concluded. Korea has sought measures to avoid a disruption in trade in the absence of equivalence agreements, including partial exemptions for certain ingredients, and announced on December 31, 2013 that there will not be assessments of penalties during a six-month "education period," which will end on July 1, 2014. Unfortunately, trade has already been considerably disrupted because Korean importers are reluctant to make purchases amidst present uncertainties. The United States has repeatedly urged

Korea to extend the current organic labeling standards or provide a provisional recognition of the U.S. National Organic Program (NOP) until an equivalence agreement can be concluded. In 2014, the United States will continue to engage Korea on this issue, including working to expedite the conclusion of the equivalence agreement between the U.S. and Korea.

UNI-PASS customs documentation – Formula Disclosure Issue

In September 2012, U.S. stakeholders alerted the United States that online Korean Customs systems required disclosure of 100 percent of all formulas and ingredients in products in order to receive customs clearance. Such disclosure risks the security of proprietary information. After engagement with U.S. authorities, Korea confirmed in December 2013 that it had removed these requirements in its online customs UNI-Pass system and now only requires the listing of the top one to two predominant ingredients. This new system has yet to be thoroughly tested in practice by U.S. stakeholders. The United States will continue to monitor this issue in 2014.

Information Technology Equipment – Electrical Safety Regulations

U.S. industry has been working closely with the Korean Agency for Technology and Standards (KATS) and the Radio Research Agency on the reorganization of safety regulations for information technology equipment. The United States has advocated for streamlined procedures that reflect the realities of contemporary manufacturing and would provide an appropriate level of safety certification for low risk information technology equipment, such as printers and computers. KATS released its final Safety Regulations rule for information technology equipment, which entered into force on July 1, 2013. These new regulations addressed many long standing U.S. concerns, including by expanding the scope of products subject to a supplier's declaration of conformity, and adopting the most current IEC standard. However, some concerns continue to be outstanding. For example, the regulation requires separate safety certification with respect to each factory's products, even for identical products produced by the same company but in a different factory. The final rule also expanded the scope of products requiring registration beyond what had been envisioned in the draft regulation, and gave companies an extremely short timeframe for implementation. Moreover, there is presently no certificate renewal process. Furthermore, despite being a Member of the IEC System for Conformity Testing and Certification of Electrical and Electronic Components, Equipment and Products Certification Bodies' Scheme (CB), KATS is not currently accepting CB reports without additional testing. Additionally, the final rule imposes burdensome labeling requirements for information that could be disclosed instead in an insert or manual. Such an adjustment is particularly appropriate for products that have small physical sizes such as cell phones. In 2014, the United States will monitor implementation as the regulation is enforced and urge Korea to allow adequate implementation time for new products as its scope increases.

Solar Panels – Testing Requirements

Korea requires solar panels to be certified by the Korea Management Energy Corporation (KEMCO) before they can be sold in Korea in projects receiving government support (which in practice means for the vast majority of sales). KEMCO's certification standards prevent certain types of thin film solar panels manufactured by U.S. industry from entering the Korean marketplace. For example, KEMCO has established a standard for thin film solar panels that can only be satisfied by panels manufactured from amorphous silicon and Copper Indium Gallium Selenide. As a result, other leading types of thin film solar panels made by U.S. firms, including Cadmium Telluride (CdTe), cannot be tested or certified under the Korean standard and thus remain shut out of most of Korea's market. The United States urged Korea at the 2012 bilateral trade consultations and at WTO TBT Committee meetings to adopt the relevant international standard, IEC 61646, without limiting its application solely to the type of thin-film solar panel its industry produces. If Korea did so, it would both facilitate trade and afford Korean consumers access to the best available technologies. In response to U.S. concerns, Korea conducted an environmental impact review on the use of cadmium in solar panels, and determined that a hazard existed for using CdTe. U.S. industry has raised methodological concerns with the studies Korea used to disqualify CdTe. The United States raised this issue with Korea in the March and October WTO TBT Committee meetings and will continue to discuss this issue with Korea in 2014.

Motor Vehicle Parts – Self-certification of Certain Spare Parts

In February 2013, Korea addressed concerns raised by U.S. industry and the U.S. Government regarding its establishment (through amendments to the Motor Vehicle Management Act and its related implementing regulations) of a requirement that five spare parts be self-certified to the relevant Korean Motor Vehicle Safety Standard (KMVSS). Concerns had been raised that the requirement would in some cases interfere with the ability to service motor vehicles certified to the U.S. Federal Motor Vehicle Safety Standards (FMVSS) in accordance with relevant provisions of KORUS. Following the submission of comments by industry and consultations with the United States, Korea clarified provisions in related administrative guidance and implemented the requirement such that this concern was resolved. As the scope of the self-certification requirement is set to expand to include additional spare parts in coming years, the United States will continue to monitor this issue and work with Korea to resolve any concerns that may arise.

Motor Vehicle Components – Compliance Testing of Sunroofs

In September 2013, in response to consumer complaints about failing sunroofs, Korean safety regulators at the Ministry of Land, Infrastructure and Transport and the Korea Automobile Testing and Research Institute conducted a product safety test of the sunroofs of all motor vehicle manufacturers whose models include sunroofs. However, both domestic and import vehicle manufacturers raised concerns that the test methodology used deviated significantly from the methodology prescribed in the relevant Global Technical Regulation developed by UNECE Working Party 29 under the 1998 Agreement and related FMVSS, and KMVSS in a manner that prejudices the test in favor of finding failure. The U.S. Government (as well as other governments) raised this issue with Korea on several occasions in the fall of 2013, including at senior levels. Korean regulators have not taken action based on the tests already conducted, and are studying the issue further, including through consultations with other countries' regulators. The United States will continue to closely monitor this issue in 2014.

Malaysia

Bilateral Engagement

The United States discusses TBT matters with Malaysia during and on the margins of the WTO TBT Committee meetings, and during TPP negotiations. The United States and Malaysia also participate actively on standards and conformity assessment issues through APEC.

Meat and Poultry Products – Halal Standards

As discussed in previous TBT reports, Malaysia requires all domestic and imported meat (except pork) to be certified as halal (produced in accordance with Islamic practices) by Malaysian authorities. Malaysian regulations require producers' halal practices to be inspected and approved for compliance with Malaysian standards on a plant by plant basis prior to export.

In January 2011, Malaysia implemented a food product standard, MS1500: 2009, which sets out general guidelines on halal food production, preparation, handling, and storage. MS1500: 2009 creates standards that go well beyond the internationally recognized halal standards, which are contained in the Codex Alimentarius. Specifically, the guidelines require slaughter plants to maintain dedicated halal production facilities and ensure segregated storage and transportation facilities for halal and non-halal products. In contrast, the Codex allows for halal food to be prepared, processed, transported, or stored using facilities that have been previously used for non-halal foods, provided that Islamic cleaning procedures have been observed.

In April 2011, Malaysia notified to the WTO its "Draft Malaysian Protocol for the Halal Meat and Poultry Productions." The protocol provides additional information and guidance on complying with MS 1500: 2009. In May 2011, the United States provided comments on the protocol and subsequently raised concerns regarding the protocol during the June and November 2011 WTO TBT Committee meetings. Following that, Malaysia scheduled mandatory audits for establishments seeking to export to Malaysia. These audits took place in September 2012. The United States received notice from Malaysian officials in April 2013 that only one U.S. establishment passed the audit, with conditional approval pending certain corrections. FSIS replied in June 2013 that corrective actions had been taken by the halal certifier and company. The company underwent a halal only review and audit in September 2013 by the Department of Islamic Development Malaysia (JAKIM) and was informed in early 2014 that it failed the audit and would have to undergo another full audit to be certified. As a result of failing the audits, these establishments are accordingly prohibited from exporting to Malaysia.

The United States raised Malaysia's halal requirements on the margins of the TPP negotiations throughout 2013, and will continue to press the issue in 2014.

Mexico

Bilateral Engagement

The United States continues to discuss TBT matters with Mexico during WTO TBT Committee meetings. The United States and Mexico also engage on standards and regulatory issues in the NAFTA Committee on Standards Related Measures, which met in February and October of 2012, and as part of the United States–Mexico High-Level Regulatory Cooperation Council, which met in August 2013.

Standards System Overhaul

Mexico is moving to consolidate all Mexican standards development organizations (SDOs) into a single Mexican SDO, AMEXNOR. U.S. stakeholders are concerned Mexico has set the ambitious goal of AMEXNOR developing between 5,000 and 15,000 standards in the next several years. It is unclear how standards development is to be funded, but Mexico has indicated it is considering expanding and codifying the current fee structure, under which all certification bodies pay ten percent of their profits into a trust. Most U.S. SDOs are already engaged with the Mexican Bureau of Standards (Dirección General de Normas, part of the Secretariat of Economy) but nonetheless; contend the process is not fully transparent. The United States and industry stakeholders will monitor standards development in Mexico to ensure that the process is fair and transparent, and allows for an opportunity to comment.

Energy Efficiency Labeling and Standby Power Usage Regulations

On September 10, 2010, Mexico published a "Catalogue of equipment and appliances used by manufacturers, importers, distributors and marketers that require mandatory inclusion of energy consumption information," a regulation on energy efficiency labeling that is applicable to a significant number of electrical and electronic products and equipment. U.S. industry stakeholders expressed their concern that implementation of the regulation would impose additional burdensome and costly labels to their exports to Mexico. The regulation became mandatory on September 11, 2011. U.S. and industry stakeholders remain concerned that this regulation sets a poor precedent and places unnecessary regulations on an extensive list of electronic products that operate at a relatively low wattage and are not regulated in the United States.

On November 14, 2012, Mexico published proposed changes to NOM-032, a regulation that would provide standby energy consumption limits, testing methods, and labeling requirements for certain electrical and electronic equipment, including digital television adapters, decoders for television reception, audio reproduction units, image reproduction equipment, and televisions with LED, LCD, or plasma displays. NOM-032 covers most of the same products as the previous aforementioned catalogue, and nearly duplicates, though does not replace it.

U.S. industry stakeholders requested a delay in the implementation of NOM-032 so that the proposed changes could be analyzed, modified, and clarified. Mexico only granted a slight delay of the implementation period of 240 days; it finalized and published the regulation in the Official Gazette on January 23, 2014.

U.S. industry is concerned that the two regulations together lead to duplicative labeling and conformity assessment regimes, resulting in unnecessary barriers to trade. U.S. industry argues that there is no real energy efficiency purpose behind the regulations and that they impose burdensome costs and procedural requirements without offering any added energy efficiency information for the consumer. Additionally, U.S. industry contends that there are likely no energy savings associated with the regulations and that NOM-032 does not consider or attempt to achieve harmony with well-established U.S. and Canadian energy efficiency or disclosure programs, such as Energy Star.

U.S. industry met with Mexico's National Commission for Efficient Energy Use (CONUEE) several times in 2013 to discuss the regulations when they were still in draft form. Although CONUEE was responsive on engaging in discussions of NOM-032 requirements, it did not alter or revise the regulation to address U.S. industry's concerns. The United States will continue to monitor this issue in 2014.

Sanitation Pipes

As noted in prior TBT Reports, the United States was concerned that Mexico's National Water Commission (NWC) had not recertified certain U.S.-origin plastic pipes for waste water systems, drinking water systems, and domestic service connections, under the Mexican recertification standard applicable at the time (NOM-001-CONAGUA-1995). According to U.S. industry, NWC had instead sought to enforce an obsolete ISO standard on high density polyethylene (HDPE) plastic pipes, that was not incorporated into the Mexican recertification standard and that relied on design and descriptive characteristics, rather than performance abilities. Furthermore, although both HDPE pipe and polyvinyl chloride (PVC) pipe – a competing product – could not satisfy the design characteristics of the ISO standard, NWC appeared to only be enforcing this standard on HDPE pipe and not PVC pipe, the latter of which is manufactured predominantly by the domestic industry. U.S. industry reported that HDPE pipe met the recertification standard contained in NOM-001-CONAGUA-199, as well as relevant performance characteristics as described in other, more up to date, state of the art international standards.

The new certification standard adopted by Mexico appeared to benefit Mexican made pipes at the expense of U.S. made HDPE pipes. The exclusion of U.S. made HDPE pipes was significant, as the collective market for plastic pipe in Mexico at its peak was well in excess of US $100 million.

The United States raised this issue with Mexico both bilaterally and in the WTO TBT Committee meetings, and requested that Mexico ensure that the standards NWC adopted applied on a non-discriminatory basis, were science-based, and were developed through transparent processes as required by the TBT Agreement. Additionally, the United States encouraged Mexico to apply the Mexican standard as written. On February 17, 2012, NWC released an amended mandatory standard, NOM-001-CONAGUA-2011, which authorized acceptance and use of standards that are utilized in the markets of Mexico's trading partners, including the United States.

Despite accepting U.S. HDPE manufacturers' requests for recertification and the completion of relevant testing, NWC stated in February 2013 that it still could not recertify HDPE plastic pipe. NWC suggested that it was unable to confirm that ASTM International is an internationally recognized standard setting body, notwithstanding the facts that the amended mandatory recertification standard did not appear to limit the standards for recertification to only those produced by internationally recognized standards setting bodies and that ASTM International is generally recognized as such a body.

In 2013, the United States continued to raise this issue with Mexico both bilaterally and in the WTO TBT Committee. As a result, in November 2013, NWC finally issued U.S made HDPE plastic pipe a three year certification. The United States will continue to monitor developments to ensure that U.S. manufacturers of sanitation pipes can compete on a non-discriminatory basis.

Peru

Bilateral Engagement

The United States discusses TBT matters with Peru during and on the margins of WTO TBT Committee meetings, and in the WTO TBT Committee of the United States – Peru Trade Promotion Agreement (TPA). The first meeting of the TBT Chapter Committee was held in September 2013.

Nutritional Labeling and Restrictions on Advertising of Food to Adolescents

On May 16, 2013, Peru enacted the Act to Promote Healthy Eating Among Children and Adolescents. This law will require a mandatory warning statement for prepackaged foods considered to have high contents of sugars, sodium, saturated fat, and trans fats. This warning statement must be displayed on the front display panel of the foods and warn potential consumers to "avoid excessive consumption" or, in the case of trans fats, to "avoid consumption" entirely. The Act also lays out restrictions with respect to the advertising and promotion of certain affected foods to children and adolescents.

Although the United States understands the public health objective that this law is aiming to address, it has raised concerns to ensure that Peru provides a reasonable timeline for the enactment of implementing regulations and to ensure that such regulations do not cause unnecessary trade disruptions and are applied fairly. For example, it appears at present that are "foods and non-alcoholic beverages in their natural states, not subject to processes of industrialization" are excluded from the scope of the Act. This could result in preferential treatment for Peru's domestic food industry, such as street vendors, whose food products may contain the same levels in sodium, sugars, and saturated and trans fat as the prepackaged foods targeted under the Act.

The United States submitted written concerns about the regulatory implementation timeline to Peru's Inquiry Point on May 9, 2013, and followed up with a diplomatic note outlining concerns on May 13, 2013. Additionally, on September 24, the Peru Prime Minister's Chief of Staff and his Healthy Eating Committee met with U.S. representatives from the Food and Drug Administration's Center for Food Safety and Applied Nutrition and the U.S. Department of Agriculture's Foreign Agricultural Service and Food and Nutrition Service. This issue has also been discussed in the framework of the United States – Peru FTA, with senior level officials in Lima, at the WTO TBT Committee in June and October 2013, with supporting interventions by Argentina, the EU, Guatemala, Mexico, and Switzerland, and on the margins of other meetings. In the WTO TBT Committee, some Members highlighted concerns that less trade restrictive approaches exist, that the present maximum daily nutrient thresholds lack a scientific basis, and that mandatory symbols and warning statements that are inconsistent with international standards might create unnecessary fear in consumers.

In 2014, the United States will continue to monitor the development of the implementing regulations, continue its discussions with the government of Peru, and explore opportunities for technical exchanges.

Moratorium on Planting Genetically Engineered Crops

On November 14, 2012, Peru published implementing regulations, for a minimum of ten years, on planting biotechnology crops. The implementing regulations, which would impose stiff penalties for noncompliance, appear to lack requisite details and guidance necessary to understand their application. Accordingly, on June 21, 2013, the United States submitted comments on the implementing regulations, noting that the level of the fines established by the proposed fine schedule appeared unreasonable and is a significant deterrent to shipping seed products to Peru. In addition, the U.S. comments noted that the fine schedule did not provide adequate clarity as to how the violations listed will be identified.

The United States urged Peru to notify the implementing regulations to the WTO at the June and October 2013 WTO TBT Committee meetings, as well as during bilateral discussions in the context of the United States-Peru TPA meeting held in 2013. The United States also asked Peru questions related to this issue during the November 2013 WTO Trade Policy Review of Peru.

The United States, other trading partners, and Peruvian domestic interests, have actively engaged with Peru on this matter. Peru is presently in the process of considering amendments to the implementing regulations. The United States will continue to carefully monitor this issue in 2014.

Labeling of Biotech Foods

On June 27, 2011, Peru notified to the WTO its Draft Supreme Decree Approving the Regulations Governing the Labeling of Genetically Modified Foods. The proposal would mandate that all genetically engineered ("GE") ingredients must be included on processed products labels. The

United States submitted comments on the notification on September 14, 2011. Peru has not responded to the comments. In 2013, Peru renewed efforts to move forward on this proposal.

The United States is concerned that this measure, by requiring mandatory labeling, would suggest that GE foods present unique dangers as compared to their conventional counterparts. Moreover, the United States is concerned that Peru's measure might undermine work being undertaken by the relevant international body, the Codex Committee on Food Labeling (CCFL). In the CCFL, Members agreed to a compendium text that can be used for the development of a labeling policy for GE foods, which states it "is not intended to suggest or imply that foods derived from modern biotechnology are necessarily different from other foods simply due to their method of production."

This issue was raised in the WTO TBT Committee by multiple Members, including the United States, at the March and June 2013 meetings of the WTO TBT Committee. At the October 2013 WTO TBT Committee meeting, Peru reiterated that the expected date of publication of the regulation had not yet been established.

The United States understands that the measure is currently undergoing an internal review by the Peruvian government. The United States is unaware presently whether Peru will allow for public comments to be submitted on any revised proposal.

The United States will continue to monitor this issue in 2014.

Russian Federation

The Russian Federation, along with Belarus and Kazakhstan, is a party to the Customs Union (CU) and the Eurasian Economic Community (EurAsEC).[44] The Eurasian Economic Commission (EEC) is the supranational body charged with implementing external trade policy for the CU.[45] Upon joining the CU, Russia transferred authority over many aspects of its trade regime to the EEC, including technical regulations, standards, and conformity assessment systems. The authority of EEC extends to the CU level as well as to the national level.

Bilateral Engagement

In 2013, the United States engaged with Russia in the WTO TBT Committee, bilaterally through the Business Development and Economic Relations Working Group (BDERWG) established under the United States - Russia Bilateral Presidential Commission, and in other fora. The BDERWG is a forum for the United States and Russia to discuss, *inter alia*, standards-related regulatory cooperation. In 2013 the United States, under the BDERWG framework, held a series of

---

[44] Kyrgyzstan and Tajikistan are also members of EurAsEC; Uzbekistan's membership in the EurAsEC was suspended in 2008.

[45] Under the terms of its WTO membership, Russia must ensure that measures taken by the EEC, to the extent that they fall within the scope of Russia's WTO commitments, are consistent with Russia's WTO Obligations.

workshops to inform U.S. industry of new opportunities and trade rights stemming from Russia's WTO membership in the area of standards, technical regulations, and conformity assessment. These outreach events culminated in a signature event, the United States – Russia Standards Forum (Forum) held in Moscow in May 2013. The Forum attracted over 300 participants from both the public and private sectors. The participants exchanged best practices and discussed proposals for further United States – Russia cooperation to better align standards systems and limit future trade barriers.

Bilateral discussions on trade and commercial ties with Russia are now suspended. If circumstances change, and if warranted, USTR will reengage in bilateral discussions on TBT issues. USTR will continue to ensure Russia's proper implementation of its WTO obligations, including with respect to TBT issues.

Transparency

The United States has continued to emphasize to Russia the importance of timely notifications to the WTO of draft technical regulations so as to enable other WTO Members to comment on them prior to their being finalized. In 2013, its first full year of membership, Russia notified 28 technical regulations to the WTO. However, it appears Russia is taking a narrow view regarding the types of measures that need to be notified. Consequently, its 28 notifications in 2013 may not reflect the full set of technical regulations or conformity assessment procedures that Russia or the EEC proposed that year. For example, Russia has not notified its new registration requirements for alcohol products. It also has not notified amendments made to its Federal Law on Circulation of Medicines; these amendments include a draft law, decree, and registration procedures concerning medical devices. Additionally, Russia has failed to notify to the WTO various other measures such as those establishing certain technical standards and regulations governing the required installation of GLONASS-compatible navigational systems in civil aircraft, as well as revisions to amendments to the EEC's regulations governing food labeling published in October 2012.

In 2013 the United States used a variety of fora to urge Russia to notify proposed technical regulations and conformity assessment procedures, including WTO TBT Committee meetings, inquiry point requests, and numerous bilateral meetings. To date, Russia has followed up by notifying some proposed technical regulations and conformity assessment procedures in a reasonable period of time. In addition, the United States has raised concerns about the comment periods provided by Russia or the EEC, as appropriate, on draft technical regulations to ensure that the United States and interested parties have adequate time to comment. In the second half of 2013 the United States has seen an improvement in the comment periods listed in Russia's WTO TBT notifications, such that there is usually a 60 day comment period and the date for final comments has not already passed when the notification is made. The United States will continue to urge Russia at the WTO TBT Committee meetings to identify and use a single inquiry point and to notify at an earlier stage proposed technical regulations and conformity assessment procedures (including proposed amendments) that may have a significant effect on trade. The United States also continues to remind Russia of its obligation to take into account comments submitted by other

WTO Members.

Food – Labeling Requirements

On July 1, 2013, new CU labeling requirements, Technical Regulation TR TS 022/2011 titled, "Food Product Labeling," went into effect. These labeling requirements mandate information on nutritional components, allergens, and GE foods. In addition, these amended labeling requirements require that products containing sweeteners must carry a warning statement that overuse will cause digestive problems, and that products with food coloring must declare that the food coloring affects a child's ability to concentrate. Russia did not notify these revisions to the appropriate WTO SPS or WTO TBT Committees. While these rules came into effect on July 1, 2013, the EEC has noted that it will allow products labeled under the previous regulations to circulate in the market until February 15, 2015. The United States sent comments with regard to the proposed revisions to the EEC in December 2012. The comments expressed concern that the revised regulations require labeling for GE products and nutritional components beyond the recommended guidelines established in the Codex General Standard for Food Labeling. Additionally, the United States noted that the requirements for the labeling of allergens in food are unclear. The revised regulations do not appear to be based on the latest scientific research nor do they appear consistent with the Codex General Standard for Food Labeling. The United States has yet to receive a response to its December 2012 comments from either Russia or the EEC. Additionally, the United States raised its concerns with Russia at the March 2013 WTO TBT Committee. In 2014, the United States will continue to engage Russia in the WTO on these and any additional outstanding concerns.

Alcoholic Beverages – Conformity Assessment Procedures, Standards, and Labeling

In December 2012, the Russian government approved Amendment No. 286-FZ which modifies Law No. 171 by setting up a new notification procedure for alcoholic beverages. On June 5, 2013, Russia's government adopted the Resolution # 474 "On Submission of Notifications About the Beginning of Turnover (sale) of Alcoholic Products on the Territory of the Russian Federation," which implemented the mandatory notification requirements established by Amendment No. 286-FZ and came into force on October 1, 2013. U.S. industry is concerned that the multiple conformity assessment procedures administered by different agencies add an unnecessary level of complexity for the sale of alcohol in Russia and are leading to increased costs and time delay.

The CU revised its "Technical Regulation on Alcoholic Product Safety" in November 2012, and included some positive changes, including removing a requirement mandating the aging of rums and reducing the size of the warning label to allow for other consumer and branding information on alcoholic containers.

However, the United States still has significant concerns with the most recent EEC draft of the "Technical Regulation on Alcoholic Product Safety," which is still under discussion within the EEC. The most recent draft of this regulation appears to impose duplicative conformity assessment procedures, administered by at least three different government authorities, all of which appear to have the same objective of data registration. Specifically the requirements call for a new alcoholic beverage notification procedure to be administered in Russia by the Federal Service for the Regulation of the Alcohol Market (FSR).

The CU "Technical Regulation on Alcoholic Product Safety," also introduces burdensome and unique requirements to label all alcoholic beverages with an expiration date, or include a label indicating that "the expiry date is unlimited if the storage conditions are observed." U.S. industry notes that the proposed requirement does not provide accurate or beneficial information for products containing more than ten percent alcohol, because these products do not expire. Furthermore, the proposed expiration date requirement appears inconsistent with international guidelines, particularly with Article 4.71(vi) of the Codex General Standard for the Labeling of Prepackaged Foods, which exempts beverages containing ten percent or more by volume of alcohol from such date marking requirements. The United States will encourage Russia to eliminate this requirement for alcoholic beverages containing more than ten percent alcohol by volume, and urge Russia to adopt international standards or guidelines for such products.

The proposed technical regulation gives rise to other issues that could affect U.S. exports of alcoholic beverages, including unclear definitions for wine and wine beverages and a requirement that whiskey be aged no less than three years. In February 2013, the United States provided comments to the EEC and will continue to work with Russia on this matter, in the context of the WTO TBT Committee.

Alcoholic Beverages - Warehousing Requirements

Russia maintains a burdensome and non-transparent licensing system for importers of distilled spirits. Importers are required to obtain an "activity" license from FSR, which covers wholesale, purchasing, supply, and storage of distilled spirits. This process is burdensome and expensive, and the license once issued is valid for only five years. The storage requirements for alcoholic beverages are set forth in Regulation Order #59. As a result of bilateral discussions that took place in 2011, Russia issued a revised regulation in 2012 that went into force in 2013 and which offered some improvements. However, issues remain. For example, the United States seeks clarification regarding the specificity of warehouse construction requirements, the stringency of warehouse inspections, and temperature controls, which appear to exceed international standards. In addition, Russian importers of U.S. products have complained in large numbers that FSR is denying their applications on spurious grounds apparently to limit the number of importers in this sector. The United States provided comments to Russia on the proposed measures in August 2012. As of October 2013, the United States has yet to receive a response from either the EEC or Russia regarding these comments. The United States also raised concerns in the WTO with Russia about these revised requirements during the November 2012 WTO TBT Committee meeting, and urged Russia to provide timely and transparent inspections because distilled spirits manufacturers continue to experience costly delays awaiting inspection approvals.

Pharmaceuticals

In January 2013, Russia released draft amendments to its Federal Law on Circulation of Medicines. To date Russia has not notified these amendments to the WTO, and the draft amendments poses several potential problems for U.S. industry, many of which stem from a lack of transparency. U.S. industry has raised concerns over Russia's definition of biologicals. U.S. industry reports that Russia is moving ahead with the definition despite these concerns. U.S. industry has also raised concerns over mandatory testing of clinical trial samples, asserting that Russia's requirements lack clarity and are too vague to implement. Lastly, Russia requires mandatory Russian patient participation in clinical trials. These requirements are often onerous for companies to meet, especially for drugs for rare medical conditions, where by definition, population samples are low.

Medical Devices

Russia's Ministry of Health Decree 1416 contains new registration procedures for medical devices, which were announced on December 27, 2012 and implemented on January 1, 2013. This time period did not provide U.S. industry adequate time to adjust and it contained unique requirements, such as Russia's non-acceptance of international clinical trials. In 2013, the United States made several interventions via bilateral meetings and through the TBT Inquiry Point to encourage Russia to notify the regulation to the WTO and provide adequate time to comment and to an opportunity adjust to the regulation. To date Russia has not responded to these inquiries, or notified the regulation to the WTO. During the BDERWG May 2013 Forum, the United States provided U.S. industry a platform to discuss this issue directly with the relevant Russian authorities. In the fall of 2013 Russia appears to have considered U.S. industry inquiries and comments, as evidenced by Russia moving back its registration deadline to January 2017.

Saudi Arabia

Bilateral Engagement

The United States engages with Saudi Arabia on TBT issues in the United States-Saudi Arabia Trade and Investment Framework Agreement (TIFA) Council and during WTO TBT Committee meetings.

Electrical and Electronic Imported Products – Transparency Concerns

On January 1, 2014, the Saudi Standards, Metrology and Quality Organization (SASO), the Ministry of Commerce and Industry and the Saudi Customs Authority implemented a new conformity assessment program called "Recognition Program on Certificates of Conformity," without notifying the program to the WTO TBT Committee or providing stakeholders notice and the opportunity to comment. In the same timeframe that this conformity assessment program was adopted, SASO also implemented IEC standards, in place of the standards for electrical products, electrical appliances, and information and communication technology developed by the National Electrical Manufacturers Association and Underwriters Laboratories, which had previously been accepted along with IEC standards. In addition, conformity assessment bodies began requesting more recent test reports, performed anywhere between two weeks to six month prior customs clearance for the shipment.

The United States has engaged Saudi Arabia bilaterally on its new conformity assessment program by sending correspondence to the Governor of SASO in December 2013, conducting bilateral meetings in January 2014 in Riyadh, and discussing the issue in the United States-Saudi Arabia TIFA Council meetings in April 2014.

In response, SASO has demonstrated a willingness to work with U.S. stakeholders by inviting participation in in-country workshops in late January 2014 to outline the requirements of the program, providing a copy of the new conformity assessment program in English, and expressing a willingness to work through individual company issues if exporters can demonstrate with evidence that products have experienced difficulty entering the Saudi Arabia market.

The United States government will continue to encourage Saudi Arabia in 2014 to establish transparent processes for stakeholder consultation with respect to this program.

Taiwan

Bilateral Engagement

The United States discusses TBT matters with Taiwan during WTO TBT Committee meetings and bilaterally on the margins of these meetings as well as under the auspices of the American Institute in Taiwan (AIT) - Taipei Economic and Cultural Representative Office Trade and Investment Framework Agreement (TIFA). A TBT working group was established during the March 2013 TIFA talks. The first TBT Working Group meeting was held in December 2013 to discuss Taiwan's changes to its chemical regulations.

Ceiling Panels – Requirements for Incombustibility Testing Methods

As discussed in the 2013 TBT Report, U.S. companies that manufacture finished interior building materials, such as ceiling panels and wood paneling, raised concerns regarding the testing method that Taiwan mandates for determining whether those materials meet applicable incombustibility requirements. According to U.S. industry, Taiwan's present measure gives U.S. ceiling tiles a lower incombustibility rating than is otherwise warranted and, in some instances, U.S. ceiling tiles unreasonably fail the test altogether. The reason the testing is problematic according to U.S. industry is that Taiwan's measure applies a variation of the ISO 5660 standard for Reaction to Fire Tests - Heat Release, Smoke Production and Mass Loss Rate, which at the time Taiwan adopted it was not complete. U.S. industry notes that a recent revision of the ISO standard incorporated additional guidelines that will ensure better and more reliable incombustibility ratings. In October 2012, USTR urged Taiwan to adopt the ISO committee's revised standard. At a technical discussion hosted by Taiwan officials for industry representatives and experts in September 2013, Taiwan told AIT that it would begin recognizing the latest ISO standards related to ceiling panel incombustibility in October 2013, although the formal announcement has not yet been made.

The United States will continue to monitor this issue in 2014 and press Taiwan to issue measures implementing this standard.

Commodity Goods – Labeling Requirements

As discussed in the 2013 TBT report, the United States raised concerns that Taiwan requires all "commodity goods" (consumer goods) to be labeled with the manufacturer's or producer's name, telephone number, and address. This measure imposes costs for firms, including the cost of developing unique labeling requirements for the Taiwan market.

In 2013, the United States raised these concerns with Taiwan, including on the margins of WTO TBT Committee meetings as well in meetings under the TIFA.

The United States will continue to monitor this issue in 2014.

Food – Mandatory Biotechnology Labeling

Since January of 2005, Taiwan has required that all food products containing biotechnology soybean or corn ingredients be labeled as "GMO" or "Containing GMO." The current labeling threshold level is five percent so products that include less biotechnology soybean or corn than that threshold do not have to be labeled. The United States is concerned about the requirements' impact on trade, and that they do not appear to be based on science. The United States has additional concerns about an amendment to Taiwan's Act Governing Food Safety and Sanitation that was passed by the Legislative Yuan in January 2014. The amendment includes language that could require additional biotechnology products to be labeled and instructs Taiwan's Food and Drug Administration (TFDA) to follow EU guidelines when implementing the labeling requirements. This is problematic because EU biotechnology regulations have lower threshold levels and do not reflect international standards. It is uncertain how this amendment will be implemented, but if TFDA enacts regulations in line with European guidelines, the amendment has the potential to increase the number of future trade disruptions. The United States will continue to monitor this issue in 2014 as Taiwan implements the new amendment.

Cosmetics – Labeling and Other Requirements

Amendments to Taiwan's Cosmetic Hygiene Control Act are under consideration. It is anticipated that after Taiwan's legislature approves the changes, TFDA will issue draft guidelines that will address requirements for product information files, product notification, good manufacture practices, product claims, and advertisements.

U.S. industry has expressed concerns that products such as toothpaste and breath fresheners would be adversely affected under the amendments. For example, it is concerned that TFDA will require that a manufacturer submit ingredient information in a product information file, which would raise issues regarding protection of proprietary information and trade secrets.

The United States will continue to monitor this issue in 2014 as implementing measures become available for comment.

Chemical Substances – ECN and NCN Programs

Importers, exporters and traders must register all chemical substances they deal with under the Labor Safety and Health Law (LSHL). Taiwan passed amendments to the LSHL in July 2013 but has not yet announced implementing regulations. Companies are required to register in order to sell, produce, import, or export chemical substances.

Taiwan's Council of Labor Affairs (CLA) started a pre-registration process in December 2009, the voluntary Existing Chemical Substance Nomination (ECN) program. The voluntary program was a simpler chemical registration program and ended at the end of 2010. The United States has engaged the CLA to make sure no trade secrets or information required by the CLA during the pre-registration process would be mishandled or improperly released. Businesses that handle chemicals, but failed to register under the ECN before December 31, 2010, are required to register those chemicals under a mandatory New Chemical Substance Notification (NCN) program. The NCN process is expected to be complex and time-consuming, but is as yet undefined, as the amended LSHL does not yet have implementing regulations. CLA may give an adjustment period for companies that did not register their substances in the ECN program, but this has not yet been decided.

Taiwan notified the WTO in July 2011 regarding the upcoming changes. Additionally, Taiwan's Environment Protection Administration revised the Toxic Chemical Substances Control Act, which protects workers in possible harmful environments, and informed the WTO TBT in March 2013. As soon as the relevant regulatory changes are made, Taiwan will ban the manufacture, export, import, and sale of any chemical substances not listed in Taiwan's chemical inventory under the ECN and NCN programs.

The United States will continue to monitor this issue in 2014 as implementing measures become available for comment.

Turkey

Bilateral Engagement

The United States discusses TBT matters with Turkey during, and on the margins of, WTO TBT Committee meetings, in meetings of the Council established under the United States – Turkey Trade and Investment Framework Agreement (TIFA), in United States – Turkey Economic Partnership Commission (EPC) talks, and in the bilateral cabinet-level Framework for Strategic Economic and Commercial Cooperation (FSECC). The FSECC is designed to reinforce the work of the EPC and TIFA and provide political-level guidance on particularly challenging commercial and economic issues.

Pharmaceuticals – GMP Decree

In late 2009, Turkey's Ministry of Health issued a "Regulation to Amend the Regulation on the Pricing of Medicinal Products for Human Use," which took effect on March 1, 2010. The regulation requires foreign pharmaceutical producers to secure a Good Manufacturing Practice (GMP) certificate based on a manufacturing plant inspection by Turkish Ministry of Health (MOH) officials, before their products can be authorized for sale in Turkey.

Although it does not oppose MOH inspection requirements for pharmaceutical manufacturing facilities, the United States has concerns with respect to certain aspects of this measure. The United States is concerned that Turkey no longer accepts USFDA GMP certifications, and that pharmaceutical producers face significant delays in meeting the inspection requirements because of the MOH's backlog of GMP inspections. In the February 2013 bilateral TIFA meeting, Turkey stated that it would consider amending its regulatory practices in order to allow MOH's review of the pharmaceutical product dossier to take place concurrently with the pharmaceutical producer's process of obtaining GMP certification. This concurrent process has not been implemented yet.

Food and Feed Products – Mandatory Biotechnology Labeling

In 2009, Turkey's Ministry of Food, Agriculture and Livestock published a regulation governing biotechnology in food and feed. The measure was not publicly announced or notified to the WTO in advance of entry into force, and contained no phase-in period. Turkey has since published several amendments to the regulation and later superseded this regulation with the enactment of the "Biosafety Law," which was notified to the WTO. This law became effective in September 2010 and mandates the labeling of ingredients derived from biotechnology in all food and feed if the biotechnology content exceeds a certain threshold, a requirement that impedes U.S. food and feed exports to Turkey. In addition, Turkey's Biosafety Law goes beyond mandatory method of production labeling, which refers to the mandatory labeling that a product or ingredient in a product was produced using biotechnology. The law requires that "GMO" labels on food contain health warnings if the biotechnology food differs from the non-biotechnology food.

This labeling requirement raises additional concerns because it appears to presume, incorrectly, that food containing biotechnology products is inherently riskier from a health perspective than its non-biotechnology food counterpart. Consequently, such health warnings could unnecessarily cause public alarm while providing no additional public health protection. For example, changes in edible oil composition could lead to health benefits, and the oil could still be as safe for consumption as similar oils. Thus, the use of health warnings in the absence of a legitimate health concern could misinform the public about food safety.

In addition to the labeling requirement, the Biosafety Law mandates strict traceability for all movement of biotechnology feed and includes onerous requirements for each handler to maintain traceability records for 20 years. The United States has engaged bilaterally with Turkey on the margins of the WTO TBT Committee meetings on issues related to Turkey's Biosafety Law. The United States will continue bilateral talks on these issues with Turkey in 2014.

Alcoholic Beverages - Labeling

Turkey notified its draft regulation on alcoholic beverage warning statements to the WTO on August 6, 2013, providing a three day comment period. The regulation requires alcoholic beverages to carry the warning statement "Alcohol is not your friend." In the U.S. comments, dated August 8, 2013, the United States requested Turkey to explain the rationale requiring this statement. Turkey has not yet responded to the U.S. request. The regulation went into effect on January 1, 2014.

The United States will continue to seek information from Turkey about this labeling requirement in 2014.

www.ingramcontent.com/pod-product-compliance
Lightning Source LLC
Chambersburg PA
CBHW080312290526
45790CB00005B/2011